MW01064053

ANDREI TARKOVSKY

INTERVIEWS

CONVERSATIONS WITH FILMMAKERS SERIES
PETER BRUNETTE, GENERAL EDITOR

Photo credit: Photofest

ANDREI TARKOVSKY

INTERVIEWS

EDITED BY JOHN GIANVITO

UNIVERSITY PRESS OF MISSISSIPPI/JACKSON

www.upress.state.ms.us

The University Press of Mississippi is a member of the Association of American University Presses.

First edition 2006

⊗

Library of Congress Cataloging-in-Publication Data

Andrei Tarkovsky : interviews / edited by John Gianvito.
     p. cm. — (Conversations with filmmakers series)
  Includes index.
  ISBN-13: 978-1-57806-219-5 (cloth : alk. paper)
  ISBN-10: 1-57806-219-5 (cloth : alk. paper)
  ISBN-13: 978-1-57806-220-1 (pbk. : alk. paper)
  ISBN-10: 1-57806-220-9 (pbk. : alk. paper) 1. Tarkovskii, Andrei Arsen'evich, 1932–1986—Interviews. 2. Motion picture producers and directors—Soviet Union—Interviews. I. Tarkovskii, Andrei Arsen'evich, 1932–1986 II. Gianvito, John. III. Series.
  PN1998.3.T36A3   2006
  791.4302'33092—dc22   2006002212

British Library Cataloging-in-Publication Data available

CONTENTS

INTRODUCTION

FEW AMONG CONTEMPORARY FILM ARTISTS inspire the degree of ardor and zeal that Andrei Tarkovsky does. In the eyes of the faithful, an encounter with virtually any of Tarkovsky's films holds the promise of awe-inspiring aesthetic transport liable to stir the innermost reaches of the spirit. To his detractors, the same films can provoke just as fervent feelings of consternation, boredom, and outright antipathy. If, however, one were to be judged by the company of one's admirers, Tarkovsky's place in the pantheon of film history would alone be secured, having earned during his career the esteem of many of the cinema's preeminent directors—Ingmar Bergman, Akira Kurosawa, Michelangelo Antonioni, Sergei Paradjanov, among a host of major artists, inside and outside the world of film.

Writing about Tarkovsky in his 1987 autobiography, *The Magic Lantern*, Bergman proclaimed that his discovery of Tarkovsky's work was akin to "a miracle. Suddenly, I found myself standing at the door of a room the keys of which had, until then, never been given to me. It was a room I had always wanted to enter and where he was moving freely and fully at ease. I felt encouraged and stimulated: someone was expressing what I had always wanted to say without knowing how. Tarkovsky is for me the greatest, the one who invented a new language, true to the nature of film, as it captures life as a reflection, life as a dream." For Kurosawa, speaking in 1987 a few months after Tarkovsky's passing, he found Tarkovsky's "unusual sensitivity . . . both overwhelming and astounding. It almost reaches a pathological intensity. Probably there is no equal among film directors alive now."[1] During the same period, an international questionnaire conducted by the French newspaper *Liberation* asked Armenian director Sergei Paradjanov, "Why do you make films?" His sole reply was "To sanctify the tomb of Tarkovsky." Having years earlier declared that his own masterpiece *Shadows of Forgotten Ancestors* would never have existed had he not seen Tarkovsky's first feature, *Ivan's Childhood*, Paradjanov would go on to dedicate his final completed film, *Ashik Kerib*, to his friend and colleague. Such veneration is scarcely limited to high art European directors.

When Steven Soderbergh deigned to remake *Solaris*, in addition to clarifying to all the disparagers that it was Stanislaw Lem's book he was remaking into a film and not Tarkovsky's film itself, his praise for the latter was unhesitating, describing Tarkovsky's version as "a sequoia" compared to his "little bonsai."[2] For the late American experimental director Stan Brakhage, whose enthusiasm for Tarkovsky's work was res-olutely unrequited (a wincing, near-comical account exists by Brakhage of his attempts to screen his own films for Tarkovsky on a hotel room wall during the Telluride Film Festival), Tarkovsky was "the greatest liv-ing narrative filmmaker." Eloquently elaborating on this declaration, Brakhage stated that "the three greatest tasks for film in the twentieth century are 1) To make the epic, that is, to tell the tales of the tribes of the world. 2) To keep it personal, because only in the eccentricities of our personal lives do we have any chance at the truth. 3) To do the dream work, that is, to illuminate the borders of the unconscious. The only filmmaker I know that does all these three things equally in every film he makes is Andrei Tarkovsky."[3]

That such accolades could be bestowed to a filmmaker whose entire feature film output consists of seven feature films over twenty years is testimony to the remarkable degree of their achievement. Indeed it was from comparable sentiments of high regard for the work, both in terms of its thematic reach and sheer "carnal impact," to borrow a phrase of Jonathan Rosenbaum's, alongside a fascination with the person responsible that the idea of putting this book together was born. Of course for anyone interested in penetrating the thought and work-ing methods of Tarkovsky, there remains no better source than his own collection of writings on cinema and aesthetic theory, *Sculpting in Time*.

It is a text I have returned to over and over again for its richness of reflection upon not only the nature and character of cinema, and the purpose of art, but for its speculations on the very meaning of life itself, Tarkovsky never being one to shy away from confronting the big questions head on. And while none of these reflections communicate as keenly or indelibly as do repeated encounters with the films themselves (the real lesson perhaps), the impulse to discover more about the artist remained.

Having appreciated the few English language interviews with Tarkovsky I'd come upon, I became curious to know what else might be going on in the interviews in all the languages I didn't know. The result of much of what I discovered is before you. While this compendium is not exhaustive of the breadth of interviews Tarkovsky gave throughout his lifetime, the attempt was to afford the reader a wide-ranging selection across the arc of Tarkovsky's career, from the first interviews following the meteoric debut of *Ivan's Childhood* at the Venice Film Festival in 1962 to the final interviews Tarkovsky granted before his untimely death in December 1986.

As a rule, Tarkovsky was wary of interviewers, telling Irena Brezna in 1984, "I have not yet been satisfied by an article that has come out after a conversation with a journalist. . . . When the journalist poses his question he is not interested in the answer, but in his notes." His apprehensions certainly had their legitimacy as the queries often put before Tarkovsky are remarkable in similitude and impoverishment. Again and again the same questions crop up—Why does he mix black and white and color? What is the difference between working in the East and the West? Who are his favorite filmmakers (a short near-unwavering list)? No doubt most frustratingly, despite continuous remonstrations against over-interpreting the meaning of his images— "If you *look* for a meaning, you will miss everything that happens . . . there's no way [a work of art] can be analyzed without destroying it"— the questions persist: What is the symbolism of water in his films? Why is the woman floating in mid-air in *The Mirror*? What is the significance of the Zone in *Stalker*? While Tarkovsky himself employs the word "symbol" in his lengthy 1969 interview with *Positif*, he would soon find the term severely limiting in characterizing the suggestive richness of a poetic image.

It's not hard to detect Tarkovsky's restlessness with the interview for-
mat when early in his conversation with Brezna he cites Goethe's
adage, "If you want an intelligent answer, ask an intelligent question."
While this confrontational joust likely had as much to do with Brezna
being female (and ironically, and in my view, tellingly, Brezna's
interview in *Tip* exemplifies more than any other interview in the
book a genuine effort at authentic communication), Tarkovsky was not
unaware of the merits of having his notions tested. "To be honest, I put
myself in the category of people who are best able to give form to their
ideas by arguing. I entirely subscribe to the view that truth is reached
through dispute," he states in *Sculpting in Time*, a book whose working
title, *Juxtapositions*, was due in its author's words to its "open-ended
structure and its avoidance of precise formulations: conclusions are to
be drawn from the juxtaposition of different theses." Nonetheless one
of the more striking aspects of the early interviews is to see so many
of the tenets of Tarkovsky's cinematic and artistic philosophy already
taking root.

Asked by Gideon Bachmann during the 1962 Venice Film Festival
to describe his theoretical principles, Tarkovsky responds that he
does "not believe in the literary-theatrical principle of dramatic
development. In my opinion, this has nothing in common with the
specific nature of cinema . . . one doesn't need to explain in film, but
rather to directly affect the feelings of the audience. It is this awakened
emotion that drives the thoughts forward." Already presaging the
formal complexity of such films as his autobiographical masterpiece,
The Mirror, he tells Bachmann, "I am seeking a principle of montage
that will allow me to expose the subjective logic—the thought, the
dream, the memory—instead of the logic of the subject." While
applicable to any one of Tarkovsky's works, one can again detect the
seeds of *The Mirror* germinating when in 1971 Tarkovsky tells Naum
Abramov, "I've noticed, from my experience, if the external, emotional
construction of images in a film are based on the filmmaker's own
memory, on the kinship of one's personal experience with the fabric
of the film, then the film will have the power to affect those who
see it."

Central to Tarkovsky's formal principles is the conviction that cinema's most distinguishing characteristic, in comparison to all other art

forms, is its literal ability to capture and preserve the flow of time.
In *Positif*'s 1969 interview on *Andrei Roublev*, the first Western interview
Tarkovsky gave on the film, it is evident that Tarkovsky is not so much
formulating stylistic preferences as he is searching out the quintessential
identity of the medium itself to which he or anyone else can then put
an individual stamp. It will no doubt strike some readers strange to
hear Tarkovsky, within the same interview, describe himself as "a
traditional director" and speaking out against experimentation in film.
"Eisenstein felt comfortable experimenting because, at the time, cinema
was at its beginning, and experimentation was the only possible path.
Nowadays, given the established cinematic traditions, one shouldn't
experiment anymore." While one might take this as evidence of a
formative stage in the evolution of Tarkovsky's thinking, the question
of experimentation comes up again in a 1984 audience dialogue in
London (included in the book as one example of several such audience
"encounters" Tarkovsky held) in relation to the editing-room wrestling
Tarkovsky undertook with *The Mirror*, attempting to determine its
form. Echoing Rodin, Tarkovsky insists that "a true artist does not
experiment or search—he finds," distinguishing the formal innovation
of his work from experimentation by dint of his assuredness in the
internal and external harmoniousness of its construction. Tarkovsky's
conception of himself as a traditionalist is perhaps only in the sense
that the real-life Andrei Roublev could be regarded so, forging innovation
within the strictures of fifteenth-century iconic painting. Alternatively
it is conceivable that Tarkovsky was being careful not to project himself
or his work as in any way revolutionary. It is important to realize that
Positif's 1969 interview was three years into the film's five-year
shelving within the Soviet Union, a situation noticeably uncommented
upon in the article. Tarkovsky's diaries are full of mentions of bureaucratic intrigue and interference, suspicions of the KGB's tampering
with his mail, monitoring his public lectures, etc., and certainly in the
pre-Glasnost USSR, any Russian artist traveling abroad could assume
some measure of surveillance. Sensitivity to these circumstances makes
for the occasional falsehood or "shaded" truth, as when he tells *Sight
and Sound* in 1981 that *The Mirror* "was in no way suppressed by the
authorities." Tarkovsky's diaries refute this, describing how the head of
the state film organization Goskino had personally prevented *The Mirror*

from going to Cannes, as do the remarks Tarkovsky made three years later in *Time Out*, following his painful decision to defect to the West, opening up in great detail to Angus MacKinnon about the extent of his difficulties working in the Soviet Union and the less-than-supportive domestic distribution of *The Mirror*.

Unreliability can spring from other motives altogether as when, following years of resistance to the endorsement of any singular interpretation of the many ambiguous elements in his films, Tarkovsky declares to Laurence Cossé in 1986 with regard to his film *Stalker* that "The Zone doesn't exist. It's Stalker himself who invented the Zone," an interpretation that seems to belie the many mysterious events that transpire in the film.

Most pronounced of the recurring refrains in the interviews, as dominates the corpus of Tarkovsky's work, is the near-messianic pursuit of nothing less than the redemption of the soul of man. "I believe . . . that an enormous task has been entrusted to art. This is the task of resurrecting spirituality." "To me, man, in his substance, is essentially a spiritual being and the meaning of his life consists in developing this spirituality. If he fails to do so, society deteriorates." "Art should be there to remind man that he is a spiritual being, that he is part of an infinitely larger spirit to which he will return in the end." Nowhere in the literature of film has one director so incessantly and insistently deployed the words "spiritual" and "spirituality" as does Tarkovsky throughout these interviews. How best to remedy mankind's "spiritual impotence" is a question that gets repeatedly prodded, poked, and examined, the discourse around which provides much of the richest and thorniest material within the book.

In his conversations about *Andrei Roublev*, Tarkovsky emphasizes the value he perceives Roublev's art having in restoring people's "faith in the future" amid a time of severe suffering and injustice. "In spite of seeing and perceiving this universe with great pain," Tarkovsky explains to *Positif*, Andrei Roublev refrains from expressing "the unbearable weight of his life, of the world around him." Instead, he "looks for the grain of hope, of love, of faith among the people of his time. He expresses it, through his own conflict with reality, not in a direct, but in an allusive manner, and therein lies his genius." Similarly, in relation to *Stalker*, Tarkovsky tells Aldo Tassone, "in this period of the destruction of faith, what's important to the Stalker is to light a spark, a belief in the heart of people." For art to fulfill its function Tarkovsky maintained that it must be put in the service of establishing a link between the individual and the Divine. Such art could be born only from the suffering and moral evolution of the artist. Tarkovsky believed, or at least wanted to believe, in the redemptive and transformative power of art. While observing, accurately I think, that, "The soul opens up under the influence of an artistic image and it is for this reason that we say it helps us to communicate, but it is communication in the highest sense of the word" (*Framework*), in a rare admission of doubt Tarkovsky tells Brezna, "Sometimes my field of work seems ridiculous to me. There are things more important. How to approach these things, how to find yourself in them, if there is a positive way in art at all, that is the question." Despite the occasional wrestling with such scruples, Tarkovsky was unable to adopt a different cast to his creations capable of rendering them more tangibly utilitarian. Nor could he envision the pursuit of a different profession, for to relinquish one's artistic calling would be a profanation of the self. ". . . [W]e should not squander our talent, for we do not have the right to consider it our own property."[4]

Not unlike Leonard Cohen's remark that being an artist isn't a decision but rather a "verdict," Tarkovsky viewed his profession as a "duty" fraught with attendant responsibility. In line with nineteenth-century Russian traditions, Tarkovsky espoused an aristocratic and discriminatory view of the artist's role as the voice and conscience of "the people," in his case specifically the Russian people, a position clearly evinced in the portrait he paints of Andrei Roublev, and one he would uphold through most of his career. However, whether it was the consequence of the repercussions of exile or evidence of his lifelong quest of self-growth, Tarkovsky seems to renounce this view when, in January 1986, he tells Laurence Cossé, "It's no longer my wish to say anything to Russians. I am no longer interested in the virtues of such prophetic stances as, 'I want to tell my people,' 'I want to tell the world.' I'm not a prophet. I'm a man to whom God gave the possibility of being a poet, meaning, of praying in another manner than the one used by the faithful in a cathedral." A few months later in late April, in a posthumously published interview with Thomas Johnson, Tarkovsky reverts back to characterizing the artist as one who "collects and concentrates the ideas of the people. He is the people's voice," having said elsewhere, "even when the artist vociferously denies this."

Of the disclosures apt to prove most disturbing to the reader are Tarkovsky's regressive pronouncements on women and their role in society. Sensitive viewers have over the years remarked on the limited portrayals of women in the films of Tarkovsky, limited not only in number and in screen time but in dimension, precisely the circumstance that led Swiss psychologist Irena Brezna, otherwise enamored of the work, to track Tarkovsky down with the specific aim of addressing this lacuna. What emerges clearly takes even Brezna by surprise as it did this reader when I first was made aware of the article. "It seems to me that woman's meaning, the meaning of female love, is self-sacrifice. That is the woman's greatness." Though Tarkovsky would explore his own capacity for sacrifice in the intervening years before his death, speaking to Brezna in 1984 Tarkovsky conflates the altruistic core of sacrifice with self-abnegation. Accordingly, for a woman to find fulfillment in life, he argues that she must be prepared to dissolve her ego into that of her beloved. Speaking at length about the "abnormality" of a single woman, Tarkovsky declares that, "Women don't understand that they only find their dignity in a male-female relationship in total devotion to the man." What's more, no allowing for or even mention is made of same-sex relationships between women, and while one might assume Tarkovsky's disapproval, this omission, along with his forcible statements on the "ideal" comportment of male-female relations, takes on a further aspect in light of surfacing reports within the Tarkovsky literature of a rumored bisexuality. That aside, though the blatant chauvinism of the remarks is hardly uncommon within Soviet society as elsewhere, one is still struck by the disconnect between Tarkovsky's perspicacity as an artist and his naiveté as a man. Scant evidence of the sage or the prophet when Tarkovsky tells Brezna that "women's social situation today is not dramatic in the way it used to be, and in a few years the balance will be reached," or during the same year when he tells an audience in London, ". . . if I were asked about my attitude toward female directors, I would not respond, for you simply need to turn your attention to the history of art." Talents are not to be squandered, that is unless you are a woman. While reference is regularly made to the poetic legacy of Tarkovsky's father, Arseni, it should be noted that his own mother, Maria Ivanovna, was said to have had a great literary gift, talents that could not have been helped by such prevailing attitudes, nor by having to raise two children alone when she and her husband divorced early in their marriage.

To his credit however, Tarkovsky did profess skepticism throughout his life of belief systems held too fast, and the interviews reveal a capacity for continuous self-examination. While acknowledging to an audience member, "You said that I am egocentric in my work: I not only don't deny this, I even admit that this is my credo," Tarkovsky, again speaking to Brezna, concedes that there could be more to this than the value of drawing from the well-springs of autobiography. "Egotism is a symptom of the fact that Man doesn't love himself, that he has an incorrect understanding of the notion of love. This is the source of the deformation of everything." Later in the same interview he confesses, "I am also my most terrifying enemy and I keep asking myself if I will besiege myself or not. This is the meaning of my life." Speaking to Hervé Guibert in *Le Monde*, Tarkovsky faults himself for his "impatience and intolerance" and again emphasizes the necessity of changing oneself before trying to change the world. "If every man was able to save himself, there wouldn't be any need to save others. We love to give advice, to instruct, while, as far as we ourselves are concerned, we overlook our gravest sins."

Despite the evident value of such soul-work, the other side of the coin for Tarkovsky is what he refers to as "the Tolstoy complex," the "ambiguous position," as he tells Gideon Bachmann, that we each find ourselves in "between some kind of spiritual ideal and the necessity of existing in this material world." This dilemma and the particular pressures it places upon the artist with regard to the social function of one's work undergoes some evolution in Tarkovsky's thinking. Far from the ringing endorsement he gives in 1973 to the East German magazine *Film und Fernsehen* for Bertolt Brecht's belief in "art as a weapon," indicating as well his support for Bertolucci's early, more politically engaged films, in his final years Tarkovsky's views resemble more those of Augustine of Hippo, his eyes cast ever more in the direction of the City of God than the City of Man. As a consequence, this shift lends the work increasingly, or at least more transparently, an eschatological dimension, as Tarkovsky's own inward search finds its echo in the thematic and formal construction of the films. The perfect offering requires the perfect form. For Tarkovsky, the crystallization of this pursuit materializes with the achievement in 1983 of *Nostalghia*.

Multiple interviewers are told of the "sudden and unexpected" discoveries that were revealed to Tarkovsky when he first beheld his creation. Speaking to Velia Iacovino in *MassMedia*, Tarkovsky states that it is with *Nostalghia* that he fully "received confirmation that cinema is a great art form, capable of representing even the imperceptible states of the soul." "I had not expected my psychological state to be capable of such clear embodiment in a film," he tells Gideon Bachmann, an embodiment incarnated in the character of Andrei Gorchakov, the homesick Russian poet who is wandering Italy researching the life of a deceased Russian composer. In the film we are told that the composer, Sosnovsky, upon returning to Russia took to drink and eventually killed himself. On-screen the character of Domenico immolates himself in an effort to arouse the conscience of society while Gorchakov, before returning to Russia, suffers an apparent heart attack upon performing an act of faith. For Tarkovsky *Nostalghia* becomes a film about "the impossibility of living," of someone suffering from a sense of powerlessness "in the face of the misery of the world." For many, it was hard not to see the film also as a foreshadowing of the personal crisis Tarkovsky would soon undergo when, shortly after the film's completion, he and his wife made the clearly agonizing decision to defect to the West.

Receiving no responses from Soviet authorities to his requests to extend his stay abroad and convinced that were he to return to Russia he'd be denied further opportunities to direct, Tarkovsky announced in July 1984 at a press conference in Milan that he would not be returning home. When asked by a reporter if he would be seeking asylum in Italy, Tarkovsky snapped back, "I'm telling you a drama. You cannot ask me bureaucratic questions. Which country? I don't know. It's like asking me in which cemetery I wish to bury my children," all of whom still resided in Russia. Ruminating over this decision a month later, Tarkovsky tells Angus MacKinnon, "I personally can't imagine how I'm going to live here. I really can't say whether I will be able to cope, to know whether I will be able to pull myself together after all this is over." When MacKinnon queries him about whether there had already been any thought given to leaving Russia during the making of *Nostalghia*, Tarkovsky denies it while suggesting that it was as much the outgrowth of his own artistic journey as having to do with any political or practical considerations. ". . . [W]hen I saw the film for the first time from start to finish, I got very frightened. The film had been creating the situation, was almost making *me*," Tarkovsky declares, adding, "I really wouldn't want to watch it again—it would be the same as someone who is ill looking at an x-ray of their illness." For Tarkovsky such words were scarcely rhetoric. The theme of the impossibility of the artist living away from his or her homeland, of the anguish of being uprooted and displaced, is one that spans generations and nationalities but runs especially strong through Russian culture. For someone like Tarkovsky the portent of these words appears to have been ineluctable. Around 2:00 A.M. between Sunday, December 28, and Monday, December 29, 1986, Andrei Tarkovsky, alone in his room at the Hartman Cancer Clinic in the Paris suburb of Neuilly, passed away at the age of fifty-four.

Diagnosed with cancer directly following completion of photography in Sweden on his film *The Sacrifice*, Tarkovsky continued to direct and oversee post-production on the film from his hospital bed. Granting but a handful of interviews, he speaks about the promise of future projects: an English *Hamlet* to be set in Monument Valley, a long-gestating project on the German romantic writer E. T. A. Hoffmann, a developing scenario around Saint Anthony. While the interviews reveal only occasional tantalizing details of how these projects might have evolved, what is certain is that, as with each of the films before, what they would surely and always be about is man's search for a meaning to his existence. It would be hard however to surmise from the evidence of these texts what measure of enlightenment Tarkovsky ultimately felt he'd yielded from his search. Still, in one of his last interviews, he says, "If he's interested in these questions, if he simply asks himself these questions, he's already saved spiritually. It's not the answer that is important."

Firmly aligned with a belief in cinema's capacity to match the highest level of man's artistic ambitions, Tarkovsky's individual search for "meaning" finally resides in the existence and enduring

achievement of the films themselves—films in whose presence I am
continually reminded of Francis Bacon's perception that "the job of
the artist is always to deepen the mystery."

As customary with all books in this series, the interviews herein
have not been edited from the form of their initial publication.
Consequently the reader will at times encounter repetitions of
both questions and answers but it is the feeling that the significance
of the same questions being asked and the consistency (or inconsis-
tency) of responses will prove of value to readers in their unexpurgated
form.

For encouraging me to contribute to the series and introducing
me to series editor Peter Brunette, I owe a debt of gratitude to critic
Gerald Peary, and to Mr. Brunette who took to the idea of a volume
on Andrei Tarkovsky unhesitatingly.

For making available to me the resources of the Institut International
Andrei Tarkovski in Paris where he serves as director, for his consistent
and careful review of the manuscript, including granting permission
to include Tarkovsky's final interview, and for his steadfast encourage-
ment throughout the lengthy gestation of this undertaking, I am
especially grateful to Charles H. de Brantes.

I must also express sincere thanks to Andrei Tarkovsky, Jr., for
granting permission for this edition of his father's words.

This book would certainly never have come to fruition without the
generous and diligent efforts of a host of translators, whose deep
interest in the material far eclipsed the humble remuneration I could
offer. These individuals are: Tim Harte, Vasiliki Katsarou, Karin Kolb,
Jake and Yulia Mahaffy, Tanya Ott, Zsuzsanna Pál, Susana Rossberg, Ken
Shulman, Deborah Theodore, and Saskia Wagner. Additional translation
review was gratefully contributed by Frank Keutsch and Alla Kovgan.

Particular appreciation goes to the editors and staff at University
Press of Mississippi—Seetha Srinivasan, Anne Stascavage, and Walter
Biggins. Their commitment to this endeavor in the face of innumerable
lapsed deadlines and their prompt and professional attention to all
facets of the project have earned my eternal gratitude and respect.

Lastly, while I might speculate that this volume could have emerged
without the unique contributions of the following individuals, it
would invariably have had a different and, I am convinced, less-rich

orientation: to filmmaker Don Levy for first unveiling the images of Tarkovsky before my eyes and to Tammy Dudman for encouraging me to take a hard and reflective look at Tarkovsky's words.

JG

Notes

1. From Mayuzumi Tetsuro, "Kurosawa: 'Tarkovsky Was a Real Poet,'" *Asahi Shimbun Newspaper*, April 15, 1987. Translated from Japanese for Nostalghia.com by Sato Kimitoshi.

2. From Geoff Andrew, "Again, with 20 Percent More Existential Grief," *Guardian*, February 13, 2003.

3. From Stan Brakhage, "Telluride Gold: Brakhage Meets Tarkovsky," *Rolling Stock* 6 (1983): 11–12.

CHRONOLOGY

1932   Born on April 4 in Zavrozhne, a village in Yurievets on the
        Volga, north of Moscow, the first child of Arseni
        Alexandrovich Tarkovsky and Maria Ivanovna Vishnyakova.
1934   Andrei's sister, Marina, is born on October 3.
1937   Arseni Tarkovsky separates from his family.
1951   Enrolls at the Institute for Oriental Languages and studies
        Arabic.
1953   Joins a geological research expedition in the Turuchansk
        region in central northern Siberia, organized by the Kirghiz
        Gold Institute.
1954   Successfully applies for a highly competitive place at the
        Moscow State Film School (VGIK), where he studies under
        filmmaker Mikhail Romm.
1956   With fellow students Alexander Gordon and Maria Beiku,
        co-directs the short film *The Killers*, based on the story by
        Ernest Hemingway.
1957   Marries fellow student Irma Rausch. In the summer, shoots
        the short television film *There Will Be No Leave Today* with
        co-director Alexander Gordon.
1958   Drafts a six-page scenario entitled *Konsentrat* (a.k.a. *Extract*)
        inspired by his experiences on the geological expedition in
        the Taiga in 1953.
1960   Begins work on his diploma film *The Steamroller and the
        Violin*, co-written with Andrei Mikhalkov Konchalovsky.
1961   Completes *The Steamroller and the Violin* and graduates
        with distinction from VGIK. The film wins first prize at the

New York Student Film Festival. Following Mosfilm Studio's decision to dismiss director Eduard Abalov from continuing to shoot the film *Ivan's Childhood*, Tarkovsky is hired to take over the project.

1962   *Ivan's Childhood* wins the Golden Lion Award at the Venice Film Festival, and Tarkovsky instantly establishes international reputation. Wins Golden Gate Award for Best Director at the San Francisco International Film Festival. Rausch gives birth to their first son, Arseni, on September 30. Acts in small role in Marlen Khutsiyev's film *I Am Twenty*.

1963   A literary treatment of *Andrei Roublev*, drafted by Tarkovsky and Andrei Konchalovsky, is accepted by Soviet authorities.

1964   The completed literary script of *Andrei Roublev* is published in the film journal *Iskusstvo Kino*. In April, Tarkovsky is given official approval to begin production. Directs a radio drama adaptation of William Faulkner's short story *Turnabout* (the basis as well for Howard Hawks's 1933 film *Today We Live*).

1966   Completes *Andrei Roublev* under the original title of *The Passion According To Andrei*. After a series of initial cuts are requested, Tarkovsky responds with a second and third edit. Despite a highly enthusiastic industry screening at the Dom Kino in Moscow, further changes are requested. Tarkovsky refuses to alter the film any further and this begins a five-year shelving of his film within the USSR.

1967   Submits a short proposal, coauthored with playwright Alexander Misharin, to Mosfilm Studios, for a project initially called *Confession*, later to be called *A Bright Day*, and *A White, White Day*, and finally *The Mirror*. Though uncredited, Tarkovsky also contributes to the script and plays a small role as a White-Guard officer in his brother-in-law Alexander Gordon's film *Sergei Lazo*.

1968   In October, Tarkovsky submits a proposal to develop a screenplay adaptation of Polish author Stanislaw Lem's science fiction novel *Solaris*. Co-writes with Artur Makarov the script for a comedy adventure film called *One Chance in a Thousand*, directed by Leonid Kotcharian and Bagrat Oganesyan.

1969   Tarkovsky continues to write the script for *Solaris* together
        with writer Friedrich Gorenstein. *Andrei Roublev* screens
        unofficially and out-of-competition at Cannes and receives
        the International Critics' (FIPRESCI) Prize.

1970   Begins filming *Solaris*. Divorces Irma Rausch in June and
        marries Larissa Pavlovna Yegorkina whom he met while
        filming *Roublev*. Their son, Andrei, is born on August 7.
        Andrei Roublev opens in cinemas in Paris.

1971   *Andrei Roublev* finally has its official Soviet theatrical release
        on December 20. Working again with Friedrich Gorenstein,
        Tarkovsky develops a script entitled *Light Wind*, an adaptation
        of a children's fairy tale by Alexander Beliaev called *Ariel*,
        about a young boy who is given the ability to fly.

1972   Gives lectures at Moscow's Advanced Screenwriting and
        Directing Courses at Goskino, something he will continue
        to do for years to earn money. *Solaris* screens at Cannes win-
        ning the Special Jury Prize, and also wins the British Film
        Institute award for best film of the year.

1973   Writes in his diary in March that he feels "the time has
        come when I am ready to make the most important work of
        my life." Begins filming *The Mirror* in July.

1975   Completes *The Mirror*. Writes screenplay *Hoffmanniana* about
        the German romantic poet E. T. A. Hoffmann.

1976   Starts rehearsals of *Hamlet* at the Lenin Komosomol Theatre.
        Begins working on the screenplay of *Stalker* in collaboration
        with Arkady and Boris Strugatsky from their short story
        Roadside Picnic.

1977   Tarkovsky's theatrical production of *Hamlet* premieres,
        starring Anatoly Solonitsyn, Margarita Terekhova, and
        Inna Churikova. Following three months of shooting in
        Estonia, Tarkovsky halts production on *Stalker* as the
        result of a technical flaw in the filmstock, dissatisfaction
        with individual crew members, and a deeper artistic
        dissatisfaction.

1978   Suffers heart attack in April. Rewrites and reshoots *Stalker*.
        For money, writes *Sardor*, a self-described "Tadjik western,"
        together with Alexander Misharin.

1979	Completes *Stalker*. Writes screenplay for *Beregis, tsmej!* (Look Out, Snake!) by Uzbekistan director Zakir Sabitov. Travels twice to Italy to begin developing a screenplay in collaboration with Tonino Guerra. The project, initially titled *Italian Journey* is the basis for *Nostalghia*. Guerra and Tarkovsky simultaneously direct a documentary essay, *Tempo di Viaggio*, on their search to discover the film. Tarkovsky's mother dies on October 5.
1980	*Stalker* screens at Cannes to wide acclaim. Returns to Italy and completes screenplay for *Nostalghia*.
1981	Travels to Sweden and attempts, unsuccessfully, to stay in the West. Begins developing ideas for a script titled *The Witch*.
1982	Begins filming *Nostalghia*.
1983	*Nostalghia* wins three awards at Cannes including the Best Director Prize which is jointly awarded to Robert Bresson for *L'Argent*. Begins working on the script for *The Sacrifice*. Directs stage production of *Boris Godunov* at Covent Garden in London under the musical direction of Claudio Abbado.
1984	Holds a press conference in July in Milan and announces his decision not to return to the Soviet Union following the refusal of Soviet authorities to grant him an indefinite stay in Italy. Tarkovsky states that if he returned home, "I would be unemployed." Moves to West Berlin at the end of the year.
1985	Travels to Sweden in the spring and films *The Sacrifice*. He is diagnosed with cancer at the end of the year.
1986	Begins medical treatment in Paris in January. His son, Andrei, and his mother-in-law Anna Egorkina arrive in Paris on January 19. His book on cinema and aesthetic theory, *Sculpting in Time*, is published. *The Sacrifice* is screened in Cannes where it receives the Special Jury Prize. Drafts a brief outline for a film called *The Destructor* about a thirteen-year-old boy dying of an incurable ailment and his love for an older woman. Around 2:00 A.M. between Sunday, December 28, and Monday, December 29, Tarkovsky passes away at the age of fifty-four.

FILMOGRAPHY

1956
THE KILLERS (UBIJTSY)
VGIK
Directors: Marika Beiku, Alexander Gordon, **Andrei Tarkovsky**
Screenplay: Alexander Gordon, **Andrei Tarkovsky**, from the short story
by Ernest Hemingway
Cinematography: Aleksandr Rybin, Alfredo Álvarez
Instructor (Cinematography class): Aleksander Galperin
Instructor (Directing class): Mikhail Romm
Cast: Yuli Fajt (Nick Adams), Alexander Gordon (George), Valentin
Vinogradov (Al), Vadim Novikov (Max), Yuri Dubrovin (First customer),
Andrei Tarkovsky (Second customer), Vasili Shukshin (Ole Anderson)
Black and white
19 minutes

1958
THERE WILL BE NO LEAVE TODAY (SEGODNYA UVOLNENIYA NE
BUDET)
VGIK
Directors: **Andrei Tarkovsky**, Alexander Gordon
Screenplay: **Andrei Tarkovsky**, Alexander Gordon, I. Makhovoi
Cinematography: L. Bunin, E. Yakovlev
Production Design: S. Peterson
Production Manager: A. Ya. Kotoshev
Assistant Director: A. Kuptsova
Camera Assistant: V. Ponomaryov

Music: U. Matskevich
Sound Engineer: O. Polisonov
Military Advisor: Lieutenant Colonel I. I. Sklifus
Directing Supervisors: I. A. Zhigalko, E. N. Foss of the Studio of
Professor M. I. Romm
Cast: Oleg Borisov (Captain Galich), A. Alekseyev (Colonel Gveleciani),
P. Lyubeshkin (Vershinin), O. Moshkantsev (Vishnyakov), V. Marenkov
(Vasin)
Black and white
47 minutes

1960
THE STEAMROLLER AND THE VIOLIN (KATOK I SKRIPKA)
Mosfilm (Children's Film Unit)
Director: **Andrei Tarkovsky**
Screenplay: **Andrei Tarkovsky**, Andrei Mikhalkov Konchalovsky
Cinematography: Vadim Yusov
Production Design: S. Agoyan
Editing: L. Butuzova
Assistant Director: O. Gerts
Special Effects: B. Pluynikov, V. Sevostyanov, A. Rudashenko
Sound: V. Krachkovsky
Music: Vyacheslav Ovchinnikov
Music Director: E. Khachachurian
Costumes: A. Martinson
Cast: Igor Fomchenko (Sasha), V. Zamansky (Sergei), Nina
Arkhanelskaya (Girl), Marina Adzhubey (Mother), Yura Brusev, Slava
Borisev. Sasha Vitoslavesky, Sasha Ilin, Kolya Kozarev, Zhenya
Klyachkovsky, Igor Kolovikov, Zhenya Fedochenko,Tanya Prokhorova,
A. Maximova, L. Semyonova, G. Zhdanova, M. Figner
Color
46 minutes

1962
IVAN'S CHILDHOOD (IVANOVO DETSTVO)
Mosfilm
Director: **Andrei Tarkovsky**

Screenplay: Mikhail Papava, Vladimir Bogomolov, based on
Bogomolov's novella *Ivan*
Additional Screenwriter: E. Smirnov
Cinematography: Vadim Yusov
Production Design: Evgeny Chernyaev
Editing: G. Natanson
Special Effects: V. Sevostyanov, S. Mukhin
Music: Vyacheslav Ovchinnikov
Music Director: E. Khachachurian
Sound: E. Zelentsova
Military Advisor: G. Goncharov
Cast: Nikolai Burlyaev (Ivan), Valentin Zubkov (Captain Kholin),
E. Zharikov (Lieutenant Galtsev), S. Krylov (Corporal Katasonov),
V. Malyavina (Masha), Nikolai Grinko (Col. Grazhnev), D. Milyutenko
(Old man with hen), Irma Tarkovskaya (Ivan's Mother), Andrei
Mikhalkov Konchalovsky (Soldier with glasses), Ivan Savkin,
V. Marenkov, Vera Miturich
Black and white
95 minutes

1966
ANDREI ROUBLEV
Mosfilm
Director: **Andrei Tarkovsky**
Screenplay: **Andrei Tarkovsky**, Andrei Mikhalkov Konchalovsky
Cinematography: Vadim Yusov
Production Design: Evgeny Chernyaev
Editing: Ludmilla Feiginova
Music: Vyacheslav Ovchinnikov
Sound: E. Zelentsova
Special Effects: V. Sevostyanov
Costumes: L. Novy, M. Abar-Baranovska
Cast: Anatoly Solonitsyn (Andrei Roublev), Ivan Lapikov (Kirill), Nikolai
Grinko (Daniel the Black), Nikolai Sergeyev (Theophanes the Greek),
Irma Rausch Tarkovskaya (Deaf-and-dumb girl), Nikolai Burlyaev
(Boriska), Rolan Bykov (Buffoon), Yuri Nikulin (Monk Patrikey), Mikhail
Kononov (Foma), Yuri Nazarov (Grand Duke/his brother), Stepan

Krylov (Bell-founder), Sos Sarkissian (The Christ), Tamara Ogorodnikova
(Mary), Bolot Eishelanev (Tartar Khan), N. Grabbe, B. Beishenaliev,
B. Matisik, A. Obukhov, Volodya Titov, Muratbek Ryskulov
Black and white, color
185 minutes

1972
SOLARIS (SOLYARIS)
Mosfilm
Producer: Viacheslav Tarasov
Director: **Andrei Tarkovsky**
Screenplay: **Andrei Tarkovsky**, Friedrich Gorenstein, based on the
novel by Stanislaw Lem
Cinematography: Vadim Yusov
Production Design: Mikhail Romadin
Editing: Ludmilla Feiginova, Nina Marcus
Assistant Directors: A. Ides, Yuri Kushnerov, Larissa Tarkovskaya
Music: Eduard Artemiev, Johann Sebastian Bach
Special Effects: V. Sevostyanov, A. Klimenko
Costumes: Yelena Fomina
Make-up: Vera Rudina
Sound: Semion Litvinov
Cast: Natalia Bondarchuk (Hari), Donatas Banionis (Kris Kelvin), Yuri
Yarvet (Snaut), Anatoly Solonitisyn (Sartorious), Vladislav Dvorzhetsky
(Burton), Nikolai Grinko (Kris' father), Sos Sarkissian (Gibarian),
O. Yisilova (Kris' mother)
Color
165 minutes

1975
THE MIRROR (ZERKALO)
Mosfilm, Unit 4
Producer: E. Vaisberg
Director: **Andrei Tarkovsky**
Screenplay: **Andrei Tarkovsky**, Alexander Misharin
Cinematography: Georgy Rerberg

Production Design: Nikolai Dvigubsky
Editing: Ludmilla Feiginova
Production Manager: Yuri Kushnerov
Lighting: V. Gusev
Assistant Directors: Larissa Tarkovskaya, V. Kharchenko. Maria
Chugunova
Music: Eduard Artemiev, Johann Sebastian Bach, Giovanni Pergolesi,
Henry Purcell
Sound: Semion Litvinov
Sets: A. Merkulov
Special Effects: Yuri Potapov
Make-up: Vera Rudina
Cast: Margarita Terekhova (Maria, Alexei's mother and Natalia, Alexei's
wife), Maria Tarkovskaya (Alexei's mother as an old woman), Filipp
Yankovsky (Alexei, age five), Ignat Daniltsev (Alexei, age twelve and
Ignat, Alexei's son, age twelve), Oleg Yankovsky (Alexei's father),
Nikolai Grinko (Ivan Gavrilovich), Alla Demidova (Elizaveta Pavlovna),
Yuri Nazarov (Military instructor), Anatoly Solonitsyn (Country doctor),
Larissa Tarkovskaya (Nadezhda Petrovna), Olga Kizilova (Redhead),
Tamara Ogorodnikova (Nanny/Neighbor/Woman at tea table)
Color, black and white
106 minutes

1979
STALKER
Mosfilm, Unit 2
Producers: T. Aleksandrovskaya, V. Vdovina, M. Mosenkov
Director: **Andrei Tarkovsky**
Screenplay: Arkady and Boris Strutgatsky, based on their story
"Roadside Picnic"
Cinematography: Aleksandr Knyazhinsky
Production Design: **Andrei Tarkovsky**
Editing: Ludmilla Feiginova
Production Support: Aleksandra Demidova
Production Manager: Larissa Tarkovskaya
Assistant Directors: M. Chugunova, Evgeny Tsimbal

Camera Operators: N. Fudim, S. Naugolnikh
Sound: V. Sharun
Assistant Editors: T. Alekseyeva, V. Lobkova
Sets: A. Merkulov
Music: Eduard Artemiev
Music Director: E. Khachachurian
Costumes: Yelena Fomina
Cast: Alexander Kaidanovsky (Stalker), Anatoly Solonitsin (Writer), Nikolai Grinko (Scientist), Alissa Freindlikh (Stalker's wife), Natasha Abramova (Stalker's daughter), F. Yurna, E. Kostin, R. Rendi
Color
161 minutes

1983
TIME OF VOYAGE (TEMPO DI VIAGGIO)
RAI TV
Directors: **Andrei Tarkovsky**, Tonino Guerra
Screenplay: **Andrei Tarkovsky**, Tonino Guerra
Cinematography: Luciano Tovoli
Editing: Franco Letti
Cast: Tonino Guerra (Himself), **Andrei Tarkovsky** (Himself)
Color
62 minutes

1983
NOSTALGHIA
Opera Film (Rome), RAI TV Rete 2, Sovinfilm (USSR)
Producers: Renzo Rossellini (executive producer), Manolo Bolognini (executive producer), Francesco Casati
Director: **Andrei Tarkovsky**
Screenplay: **Andrei Tarkovsky**, Tonino Guerra
Assistant Directors: Norman Mozzato, Larissa Tarkovsky
Cinematography: Giuseppe Lanci
Production Design: Andrea Crisanti
Editing: Erminia Marani, Amedeo Salfa

Assistant Editor: Roberto Puglisi
Set Dresser: Mauro Passi
Special Effects: Paolo Ricci
Music: Verdi, Wagner, Beethoven, Debussy
Musical Consultant: Gino Peguri
Costumes: Lina Nerli Taviani, Annamode 68
Sound: Remo Ugolinelli
Sound Re-recording: Filippo Ottoni, Ivana Fidele
Sound Effects: Massimo Anzellotti, Luciano Anzellotti
Cast: Oleg Yankovsky (Andrey Gorchakov), Erland Josephson
(Domenico), Domiziana Giordano (Eugenia), Patrizia Terreno
(Gorchakov's wife), Laura De Marchi (Woman with towel), Delia
Boccardo (Domenico's wife), Milena Vukotic (Town worker), Alberto
Canepa (Peasant), Raffaele Di Mario, Rate Furlan, Livio Galassi, Piero
Vida, Elena Magoia
Color, black and white
126 minutes

1986
THE SACRIFICE (OFFRET)
Swedish Film Institute (Stockholm). Argos Films (Paris). In association
with Film Four International, Josephson & Nkyvist, Sveriges
Television/SVT 2, Sandrew Film & Teater. With the participation of the
French Ministry of Culture.
Producers: Anna-Lena Wibom (executive producer), Katinka Faragò
Director: **Andrei Tarkovsky**
Screenplay: **Andrei Tarkovsky**
Production Manager: Goran Lindberg
Cinematography: Sven Nykvist
Production Design: Anna Asp
Editing: **Andrei Tarkovsky**, Michal Leszczlylowski
Editing Consultant: Henri Colpi
Camera Operators: Lasse Karlsson, Dan Myhrman
Special Effects: Svenska Stuntgruppen, Lars Hoglund, Lara Palmqvist
Music: Johann Sebastian Bach, Swedish and Japanese folk music
Costumes: Inger Pehrsson

Make-up: Kjell Gustavsson, Florence Fouquier
Sound: Owe Svenson, Bosse Persson, Lars Ulander, Christin Lohman,
Wikee Peterson-Berger
Cast: Erland Josephson (Alexander), Susan Fleetwood (Adelaide), Valérie
Mairesse (Julia), Allan Edwall (Otto), Gudrún Gísladóttir (Maria), Sven
Wolter (Victor), Filippa Franzén (Marta), Tommy Kjellqvist (Little Man),
Per Källman (Ambulance man), Tommy Nordahl (Ambulance man)
Color, black and white
149 minutes

ANDREI TARKOVSKY

INTERVIEWS

Andrei Tarkovsky:
I Am for a Poetic Cinema

PATRICK BUREAU / 1962

HE'S THIRTY YEARS OLD. He was born on the shores of the
Volga, but his family is from Moscow. A family of poets, of intellectuals,
very preoccupied with painting and music. Tarkovsky can be classified
within the ranks of what we call "the Soviet New Wave." But how is it
that he came to cinema?

"After having studied for a time the problems of Eastern civilization,
I spent two years as a worker in Siberia in the field of geological
research and then returned to Moscow. There I enrolled in the Moscow
Cinematographic Institute where I was the student of Mikhail Romm.
I received my diploma in 1961. I had directed two shorts, one of them
was *The Steamroller and the Violin*. In summary it was an exercise in
eclecticism before going to work at Mosfilm and directing *Ivan's
Childhood*."

PB: *What did you want to express in your first film?*
AT: I wanted to convey all my hatred of war. I chose childhood
because it is what contrasts most with war. The film isn't built upon
plot, but rests on the opposition between war and the feelings of the
child. This child's entire family has been killed. When the film begins,
he is in the midst of the war.

From *Les Lettres Francaises*, no. 943 (September 13–19, 1962). Translated from French by
Susana Rossberg and John Gianvito.

PB: *Have you put into the film some part of your own personal experience?*
AT: Truly no, since I was very young during the last war. I therefore translated the feelings that I had experienced because this is a war we are unable to forget.

PB: *What were your shooting conditions?*
AT: I shot for four months during the summer of 1961 and devoted nearly two months to editing. The film cost 2.5 million rubles which is a medium-sized budget.

PB: *Can it be said that you are part of the new wave of Soviet filmmakers?*
AT: It's possible but I hate these schematic definitions.

PB: *I dislike them as much as you but I'm trying to situate you in the stream of Soviet production. If you prefer, can you tell me what Russian cinema represents for you? And in what ways do you feel most connected to it?*
AT: There are nowadays in the USSR diverse tendencies which pursue parallel paths without upsetting one another too much, and in terms of this I am able to position myself. For example, there is the "Gerasimov" tendency that looks, above all, for truth in life. This tendency has had a great deal of influence and a large following. Two other tendencies are beginning to define themselves and appear to be more modern. One can trace their origins to the period of the 1930s. But it was only after the Twentieth Congress that they were able to free themselves and to develop, that their locked up energies were able to be released. What then are these two tendencies? On one side, it is "poetic cinema," illustrated by Chukrai's *Ballad of a Soldier* and *The Man Who Followed the Sun* by Mikhail Kalik, which one could compare to *The Red Balloon* by Lamorisse but which in my opinion is far superior. I believe I could be situated within this tendency of poetic cinema, because I don't follow a strict narrative development and logical connections. I don't like looking for justifications for the protagonist's actions. One of the reasons why I became involved in cinema is because I saw too many films that didn't correspond to what I expected from cinematic language.

On the other hand, there is what we in the USSR call the "intellectual cinema" of Mikhail Romm. In spite of the fact that for a time I was his student, I can't say anything about it because I don't understand that kind of cinema.

All art, of course, is intellectual, but for me, all the arts, and cinema even more so, must above all be emotional and act upon the heart.

PB: *Do you think that the evolution of the young Soviet cinema is parallel to the poetic movement?*

AT: I don't think so because Soviet poetry is developing upon a different ground than that of the young cinema. We certainly have points in common and also the same age, but personally I don't agree very much with Yevtushenko whose point of view should be expressed more directly and more emotionally. I don't know what the results are going to be, but I would like to choose the path of feelings. Compared to the emphaticism of Yevtushenko, I prefer conciseness, a more concentrated mode of expression.

PB: *Is there a film crisis in the USSR at this time?*

AT: Absolutely not. The cinemas are full for every screening, and we even lack enough screening rooms. One of the reasons we have no crisis is that there is no competition from television. The function of television is different, and less important, than the function of film. Surely TV hasn't yet found its path.

Even before I could ask him the ritual question that closes every interview, Andrei Tarkovsky spontaneously told me about a project that is dear to him.

AT: A film about Andrei Roublev, a fifteenth-century Russian icon painter. There are virtually no documents about his existence, we only know a couple of his works, and one of them, *The Trinity*, that can be found in the Tretjakov gallery in Moscow, gave me the idea for the film. Upon seeing this icon, I was able to imagine life in this terrible time, the time of Dimitri Donskoi. The issue is not to make a historical film, but to reveal the talent of a painter whose work has acquired enormous importance over time. I am trying to make the *fuga temporum* palpable, to show the relationships between time and the artist: how a man, starting with the abstract idea of the Trinity, was able to make us feel all of human fraternity. In any case, at no moment do I forget reality.

Encounter with Andrei Tarkovsky

GIDEON BACHMANN/1962

We recently reported on Ivan's Childhood, *the Soviet film that caused a sensation at Karlovy Vary and Venice. With this film, Tarkovsky (like all of the younger Soviet directors a graduate of VGIK, the Moscow Film Academy) became a member of a group of innovators in Russian cinema. Gideon Bachmann writes about a personal encounter with Tarkovsky, which, having taken place during the turbulent Venice Film Festival, had to be somewhat informal.*

HE IS A NERVOUS MAN in his thirties who looks much younger; his shirt is open, a scarf under the collar around his neck, according to the Russian style. The hair above his twitching forehead is short. He has strong, broad cheekbones and thin lips, which he often presses together, above a prominent chin. During the press conference he gestures wildly, ignoring the microphone in his hands, which makes the volume of his voice rise and fall. He performs a sort of dance on the stage of the Festival Palace as he attempts to answer the journalists' questions despite the poor translation by illustrating the meaning of his words with body language. The talk is of accusations that he is a formalist, a charge leveled, interestingly, by both the far right (*Il Borghese*) and the far left (*Mondo Operaio*) of the Italian press. It seems this is not the first time Tarkovsky has heard this accusation, yet he is immune to criticism that seems groundless to him. He pays scant attention to it

From *Filmkritik*, no. 12 (December 1962). Reprinted by permission of author. Translated from German by Tanya Ott and Saskia Wagner.

and instead tries to talk about other ideas that he apparently has had about his work. He wants (as he states innocently in front of these seasoned festival-goers, who are used to reacting to this kind of simplicity with skeptical derision) to re-introduce poetic imagery to filmmaking. Impatiently bypassing the political introduction by the head of the delegation, he says that Russian cinema, especially in the 1930s, had built a tradition that represents a responsibility, and that he sees it as his job to do this tradition justice. He rattles through the names as if in an introductory course: Pudovkin, Eisenstein, Dovzhenko; the great Russian cinema of the pre-war era. Pressed by the journalists, he admits that the 1920s, especially from a poetic point of view, were more significant for Russian cinema, yet he demonstrates tactfulness by mentioning *Chapayev*, which is from the '30s, as an example of his theory. The insufficient three-step translation causes him to become increasingly impatient, and he talks more, while being understood less.

Therefore, we try to have a private meeting. We finally have the opportunity during the late afternoon, between the Russian cocktail hour and dinner. But new problems arise as the translator succumbs to the effects of vodka shortly after the introduction. We then find out that Tarkovsky understands some English, and with the help of our minimal knowledge of Russian, we manage to at least ask our questions in an understandable way. Then, we just let him talk. His flow of words can later be translated from the tape-recorder.

GB: *Would you consider yourself a part of the Russian "New Wave"?*
AT: In terms of a special trend in the USSR, there is no "New Wave." Being in my thirties, I simply belong to the youngest generation of Russian filmmakers. My generation tries very seriously to explore the relationship between form and content. This issue was never addressed thoroughly enough in Russian cinema, and my generation is the first to really think about the fact that it can lead to vulgarization if the topic has too much influence on the form.

GB: *One can sense a powerful formal change in Russian film over the past two years. What is behind this loosening up?*
AT: The search for a new formal structure is always determined by thoughts that demand a new means of expression. For example, it is

impossible today to see the war through the eyes of those who consciously experienced it. In my film, I try to see it through the eyes of a person of my age. I am judging the past from a contemporary point of view. I am illustrating what I could have experienced if I had taken part. I have witnessed how war can mentally cripple someone. And today, the problem of war has to be solved again by my generation; it is the most relevant of all topics, but our new point of view forces us to find new forms for it.

GB: *Regarding the question of composition, there must be so many polemics surrounding you, given the fact that there are so many new and varied things being produced at the moment.*

AT: There is much discussion in the USSR at the moment about whether it is at all possible to express contemporary problems through the essence of the individual. This is the subject of our polemics: can the "I" represent the community? At the same time, dealing with that problem helps our younger artists search for their own essence. In the past, this search was very hard. You could not simply attempt to express yourself. I do not need to tell you why that was so hard. But now there are major changes going on in the USSR, enabling artists, for example, to represent the general through the personal. Therefore there is no "New Wave," but rather as many styles as there are artists.

GB: *It is very unusual that the USSR would send a debut film to Venice, especially one that has been so groundbreaking. Was there a lot of discussion about the selection?*

AT: Oh yes. As soon as the film was done, we showed it to our older colleagues, including Mikhail Romm. After the screening he told me that for him, the film represented a revelation of the direction young people are going in. In general, the older generation was more sympathetic towards the film than I had expected. I know that they have a different view of things. They are interested in other forms, and these topics do not excite them as much as they do us, the younger generation. Still, my older colleagues, like Romm, Kalatozov, and Urusevsky, congratulated me and told me that the film carried on the traditions of Soviet cinema. Yet there were extensive discussions about the question of form. But I found that these discussions were largely unfounded and superficial. This film was a great inner struggle for my co-workers and me, and we weren't happy to see that people were talking about our work lightly and in a theoretically groundless way. We want to be treated seriously and with respect. The film has since found so many admirers that I think I was successful with it.

GB: *Do you already have an idea for your next film?*
AT: I am planning to make my next film about Andrei Roublev, the great Russian painter of the fifteenth century. Here is the topic that interests me: the personality of the artist in relation to his times. As a result of his natural sensitivity, a painter is able to more deeply grasp his era and to reproduce it more completely than anybody else.

It is not going to be a historic or a biographical film. What fascinates me is the process of the artistic maturity of the painter, the analysis of his talent. Andrei Roublev's art represents the pinnacle of the Russian Renaissance; he is one of the outstanding figures in the history of our culture. His art and his life both offer rich material.

Before we started writing the script we researched historical documents and records, mostly to be able to decide what we would not use in the film. For example, we are less interested in historical stylization through costumes, settings, and language. The historical details are not supposed to divide the attention of the viewer, only to convince him that the action really takes place in the fifteenth century. Neutral set decorations, neutral (yet convincing) costumes, the landscapes, the modern language—all this will help us to talk about the most essential aspects, without distracting the audience.

The film will consist of several episodes that are not directly logically connected to one another. Rather, they are connected internally through ideas. We do not yet know in which sequential order the novellas will be joined; maybe chronologically, maybe not. We want to organize the episodes according to their implications for the evolution of Roublev's personality, so that they build on each other dramatically during the birth of his idea for the magnificent icon of the Troiza (Trinity). At the same time, we want to avoid any traditional dramaturgy, with its canonical isolation, its logical, formal schematism, because it often prevents full expression of the richness and complexity of life.

GB: *Could you elaborate on your basic idea of the artist's personality in relation to his era?*

AT: Let's call it the dialectics of personality. Every event that human beings experience becomes part of their character, part of their outlook, part of the people themselves. Therefore, the "events" in the film are supposed to form not just the background in which the "hero" is placed. Films about artists are often made in the following way: the protagonist observes an event. Then he starts to think about it in front of the audience, then he expresses his thoughts in his work. In our film, in no scene will Roublev paint his icons. He will simply be living and will not even appear in all of the episodes. And the last part of the film, which we plan to shoot in color, will be dedicated to Roublev's icons. In fact, we will show them in a detailed way, as they would be displayed in a documentary. The appearance of every icon onscreen will be accompanied by the same musical theme that will have played during the corresponding filmed episode of Roublev's life symbolizing the period of development of the idea for that icon.

We are bound to this structure for the film by its intended purpose: we want to show the dialectics of the character, to explore the life of the human spirit.

GB: *You keep saying "us"; who else is going to work on this film?*

AT: The same team will work on the film about Roublev that assisted me on *Ivan's Childhood*: cinematographer Vadim Yusov, art director Yevgeny Chernyaev, and composer Vyacheslav Ovchinnikov. I am already convinced that these people and I think in a similar manner.

GB: *Are there any theoretical principles in your work that you could summarize in a few words?*

AT: The only manner in which a creative idea should enter the awareness of the audience is via the trust the creator has in his audience. A dialogue in which audience and creator are equal partners has to be developed. There is no other approach; even if something is absolutely self-evident to the creator it is entirely wrong to try and force this into the audience's mind. The aesthetic ideas generated by the viewers have to be accommodated, but one must never compromise and neglect the duty to create modern cinema. In no case should one concede to the tastes of the more backward viewers.

I do not believe in the literary-theatrical principle of dramatic development. In my opinion, this has nothing in common with the specific nature of cinema. There are too many characters in today's films that only serve to explain the circumstances of the events to the viewer. One doesn't need to explain in film, but rather to directly affect the feelings of the audience. It is this awakened emotion that then drives the thoughts forward. I am seeking a principle of montage that will allow me to expose the subjective logic—the thought, the dream, the memory—instead of the logic of the subject.

I am looking for a method of composition that stems from the situation and the psychic condition of the human being, meaning that it should result from the circumstances that objectively influence human behavior. This is the first requirement for reproducing psychological truth.

The Burning

IN THE ANDRONNIKOV MONASTERY IN MOSCOW is a
cell where Andrei Roublev lived out the last years of his life. Today, the
Museum of Ancient Russian Art, dedicated in his name, is located here.
In the courtyard of the monastery, the director Andrei Tarkovsky has
shot several episodes of a film dedicated to the artist and named after
him. These are only a few parts from a long, almost three-hour picture,
which has been extensively and painstakingly planned and just as
extensively and painstakingly shot. There has been so much work,
stress, disappointment, and hope. There have been so many ideas,
fears, and joyful realizations . . . We stood in the courtyard and looked
over the sets, made so skillfully that they were hard to discern from
the original buildings.

And here, surrounded by the real and the reconstructed antiquity,
where the fifteenth and twentieth centuries have merged, we thought,
once again, about how history and the present-day interrelate in this
large and complex film. We say once again, because these thoughts (of
course, not just for us) first arose immediately upon the publication of
the screenplay, written by Andrei Konchalovsky and Andrei Tarkovsky.
At that time, together with the pleasure of reading the wonderful prose
(for the screenplay is valued as an independent literary work), arose
several questions, that only the director himself could answer. Now
we had the chance to ask them.

"Why specifically Roublev?," we asked Andrei Arsenivich.

From *Ekran*, 1965, 154–57. Translated from Russian by Jake Mahaffy and Yulia Mahaffy.

"Because," answered the director, "Roublev is a genius. In other words, he's a person seeing the world with a painful keenness, reacting with utmost sensitivity to everything he encounters, to things that other people, after seeing so much and getting used to so much, pass by indifferently, not noticing. And also, because an artist is always the con-science of society. But that's only half the answer. The character of Roublev attracted us because there is little about him that is known with any certainty. And that means, that in creating the character, we were absolutely free to construct Andrei's personality without being bound either to a biography of Roublev or to established preconcep-tions about him."

Q: *Therefore, history in and of itself, interests you least of all. So, this picture about Roublev is a picture saturated with the ideas of our time?*
T: In my opinion, history in and of itself, cannot be a subject for art. I can't comprehend films in which the stylization of history turns into an escape from the present-day. Of course, it's not about making direct references and associations. All sorts of hints and a veiled defiance of authority make a film neither contemporary nor profound. It's too petty a task. It's much more important, it seems to me, to use the his-torical material only as an excuse to express your own ideas and create contemporary characters. And it will be very sad if we are to be judged primarily from scientific, historiographic, or art historical points of view. Such a view on art can kill even Shakespeare who, whether he wrote about the real Roman, Caesar, or the legendary Dane, Hamlet, always remained true to the issues of his age.

Q: *Although there are hardly any informational sources on Roublev's life, and what sources there are, are very meager, the epoch recreated in the film has been studied fairly well. There is a voluminous literature related to that time period, and that literature has been thoroughly studied by the director. We saw the sets, not only here, but also in Vladimir, and all of them are incredibly exact. The same fidelity exists in the costumes, in the domestic utensils, in the appearance of the monasteries, peasant homesteads, and the palaces of princes.*
T: Here, we tried not to make mistakes. But no exoticisms, nor any stylization is acceptable to us. That includes the stylization of language.

The characters in this picture speak the modern Russian language that everyone can understand, without either archaic expressions or the newest terminology. Nothing should impede perception, or distract the viewer from the main thing.

Q: *When we were on the set of* Pharaoh, *we discussed this same subject with Jerzy Kawalerowicz. He thinks that in a film with a historical plot, it's not as important to have scrupulous fidelity to an epoch as to divorce yourself from what he calls an "automatism of movement" that's inherent to a modern person. Gaits, gestures, and mannerisms of the characters in his films differ sharply from ours.*

T: I think that this diffuses the viewer's attention, leading him away from the primary thing. Once again, I repeat: In this picture about Roublev, we tried in every way to make sure the viewer would not notice anything exotic.

Meanwhile, it was getting time to film a scene and on the set it was, as always, getting hectic. Hiding away from the bustle, a tall, thin monk entered the bus where we were sitting and sat silently in the corner. It was the main character of the film, himself, played by the actor Anatoly Solonitsyn from Sverdlov.

Q: *Why after so many screen-tests did Tarkovsky choose him specifically?*

T: Of course, most importantly, I sensed in him the most accurate correlation to the Roublev that I imagined. But there is still another reason. In choosing the actors I wanted to step away from those principles of type-casting which often lead to cliché. We paid the least amount of attention to how they look, and we were most interested in the inner correlation between the character in the film and the artistic temperament of the person who was intended to play the role.

Q: *So what is he like, Andrei Roublev, that he is so dear to you, and why should he be dear to us, the viewers?*

T: At a time when the life of the people was hopeless, when they were oppressed by a foreign yoke, by injustice, by poverty, Roublev expressed in his art a hope, a faith in the future. He created a high moral ideal. As a rule, icons in his time were cult objects with conventional representations of the saints, nothing more. With Andrei it was different. He strove to express an all-embracing harmony of the world, the serenity of the soul. The idea of searching for this noble peace, eternity, and harmony of the soul, an idea he dedicated his whole life to, made it possible for him to create masterpieces, which will always remain relevant.

In the film, we lead him to purification through suffering, finding joy in passion, which he had rejected earlier. The main thing that I want to express in my film is the burning of a person in the name of an all-consuming idea, an idea that possesses him to the point of passion.

Q: *That's the same type of protagonist as in* Ivan's Childhood.

T: And the protagonist of Stanislaw Lem's novel, *Solaris*, which I want to adapt, and the protagonist of the well-known story by Freidrich Gorenstein, *House with a Little Tower*. A protagonist who, in the adaptation I'm working on now, becomes a mature human being and dedicates himself to one goal: a search of the past and a liberation from it. See, at least I'm consistent.

The Artist in Ancient Russia and in the New USSR

MICHEL CIMENT, LUDA SCHNITZER, AND JEAN SCHNITZER/1969

DURING THE MOSCOW FILM FESTIVAL Andrei Tarkovsky was nowhere to be seen. The resounding Cannes presentation of *Andrei Roublev,* arranged by the French distributor to the displeasure of the Soviet officials, could but force him to undertake this wise move. Any publicity made around his name would have only led to questionable ambiguities or to an unscrupulous exploitation. The following conversation is the only one he had with a foreign magazine. Since his film isn't mentioned in the Soviet press, we can say that these declarations, recorded on a tape recorder, have an absolute, unique value. A few Moscow conversations were sufficient for us to measure the importance of *Andrei Roublev* for the enlightened community and the prestige with which Tarkovsky is held by filmmakers of all generations. His intellectual honesty, his seriousness, the scope of his inspiration, the patient work that took up nearly seven years of his life, have earned everyone's respect. His work is the standard for every filmmaker who tries to open up new ways. Even as it speaks to everyone, it expresses first and foremost the difficulties and aspirations of an entire intellectual milieu. We could not have wished for a better introduction to future reflections on Soviet cinema that will appear in a forthcoming issue, than these remarks.

From *Positif*, no. 109 (October 1969): 1–13. Reprinted by permission. Translated from French by Susana Rossberg.

MC: *How did you become a filmmaker?*

AT: I was born in 1932, on the banks of the Volga, in my grandparents' house, where my parents had gone to take a rest. After which . . . a mass of uninteresting details. I finished Music School, I painted for three years—all this during secondary school.

Then the war started. We returned to the place where I was born. When the war ended, I finished my secondary studies. In 1952 I entered the Institute for Oriental Languages, where I learned Arabic. I left the Institute after two years because I became aware of the fact that it did not suit me. . . . Do you know Arabic? It's a mathematical language. Everything in it obeys laws wherein you introduce root words in order to obtain a new declination, or a new grammatical state. All of this was not for me. Then I worked for two years in Siberia, doing geological prospecting. Then, in 1954, I entered VGIK, in the workshop of Mikhail Ilych Romm. I finished VGIK in 1960. My thesis work was *The Steamroller and the Violin*, which is important for me because that's where I met my director of photography Vadim Yusov and the composer Vyacheslav Ovchinnikov, with whom I continue to work.

LS: *Did they graduate from VGIK with you?*

AT: No. Yusov graduated well before me, and Ovchinnikov was finishing his studies at the Moscow Conservatory. In 1962, I finished *Ivan's Childhood* and, together with Andrei Konchalovsky, I started to think about the screenplay of *Roublev*. We then wrote it, and the filming was finished by the spring of 1966. Right now, I just finished a screenplay based on a novel by Polish writer Stanislaw Lem, a science fiction piece whose title is *Solaris*. I handed it over to the Artistic Counsel, which will deliberate about it. I intend to start directing this film soon.

JS: *In order to determine the type of science fiction more precisely, is it a sort of social forecasting?*

AT: No, the film does not contain any social problem. It deals with the relationship between morality and knowledge.

JS: *It is known that* Roublev *provoked an ardent polemic, stemming from the pretext that historical inaccuracies had made their way into your film. Among other things, it was maintained that Roublev and Theophanes the*

Greek couldn't have worked together because they had lived a century apart. However, specialized works seem to confirm your assertions. Assuredly, we know little about Roublev's life. Did you gather and extrapolate historical materials concerning Roublev?

AT: I hesitate to speak about the historical accuracy and inaccuracy. We stirred up a mountain of documents, trying to come as close as possible to historical truth. We also had many advisors who saw what we were doing and who accepted our point of view without reservations. I can, however, tell you what I think about this: it isn't a question of historical inaccuracies, but of the fact that, while shooting the film, we somewhat shifted our emphasis in accordance with our intentions. Our aim wasn't to minutely expose all of the events that took place at the time. Our purpose was to trace the road Roublev followed during the terrible years wherein he lived, and to show how he overcame his epoch. For this reason we opted for a certain condensing of events. The emphasis we introduced was crucial in order to underline the difficulties Roublev had to overcome, which were primarily moral. Without this, there wouldn't have been the feeling of victory at the end, which is the raison d'etre of the film.

Another thing—Engels expressed a marvelous idea: the level of a work of art is as high as the idea it expresses is deeply buried, well hidden. That is the course we chose to take. We worked at drowning our idea in the atmosphere, in the characters, in the conflicts between different characters. And that is maybe why in our case pure, direct History, though it doesn't get relegated to the background, dilutes itself in the atmosphere of time. This may be an unusual way to approach historical material, and it's what has led certain people to talk about historical inaccuracy. I believe herein lie the origins of the misunderstanding.

MC: *In* Roublev *there is an almost systematic use of the intricately choreographed sequence shot, which is the opposite of Eisenstein's manner of filming. Eisenstein has often, erroneously, been cited in relation to your film.*
AT: What can I say about that? I profoundly respect S. M. Eisenstein, but it seems to me that his aesthetics are foreign and, frankly, not applicable to me. In *Potemkin* and Eisenstein's first works, his attachment to detail and the "pathetic realism" of his shots, speak to me, but not his editing principles, his "editing pathetics." In his last films, like

Alexander Nevksy and *Ivan the Terrible,* which were shot in studios, he's only registering previously drawn sketches on film. This doesn't suit me at all, because I have a completely different concept of the editing process.

I consider cinema to be the most realistic art in so far as its principles are based on its identification with reality, on the fixing of reality in every separately filmed shot—something we find in Eisenstein's first films. As for the parallel that has been established between Eisenstein and me, that's the business of film critics. I have trouble judging my film from that point of view. I believe that we have to part our ways, Eisenstein and I, concerning the principles of pictorial realism and editing. The specific character of cinema consists in pinning down time. Cinema operates with time that has been seized, like a unit of aesthetic measure which can be repeated indefinitely. No other art possesses this capacity. The more realistic the image, the nearer it is to life, the more time becomes authentic—meaning, not fabricated, not recreated . . . of course it is fabricated and recreated, but it approaches reality to such a point that it merges with it.

As for editing, my principle is the following. The film is like a river; the editing must be infinitely spontaneous, like nature itself. That which forces me to go from one shot to another by means of editing is not the desire to see things from closer up, nor to force the spectator to hurry up by introducing very short scenes. It seems to me that we are still in the bed of time, meaning that, in order to see nearer, we don't have to see things in close-up—that's at least my opinion. And accelerating the rhythm doesn't mean making shorter sequences. Because the movement of the event itself can be accelerated and can create a new sort of rhythm, and a long shot can give the impression of being detailed—that depends on its composition. Which is why, in these two specific instances, one is not close to Eisenstein at all. Furthermore, I do not consider that the essence of cinematography is the collision of two scenes, a collision that should give birth to a third notion, as Eisenstein used to say. On the contrary, the nth shot seems to me to be the sum of the first, the second, the third . . . fifth, tenth . . . and of the shot "nth-1", meaning the sum of all shots preceding the nth. Thereby we create the sense of a shot, in relationship to all the shots that have preceded it. That is my editing principle.

For me, the isolated shot, by itself, is senseless. It acquires its completeness only through the fact that it is part of a whole. Better yet—it already contains that which will happen after it. It is often incomplete—that is how it has been filmed—because one is thinking about what will be happening after it. I know that in one of his last letters, if not the last one (Professor Svortzov, of the film direction faculty of VGIK, told me about it), Eisenstein renounced his editing principle and his manner of filming scenes of a theatrical nature, in the name of new ideas which are very close to mine. But he didn't have time to apply them, he was prevented by death.

MC: *With Eisenstein, in* Ivan *or even* Nevsky, *the character is at the center of the film. It seems to me that in* Roublev *the world is as if seen by the painter, and that, finally, the society in which Roublev lives plays a role at least as large as Roublev himself. That seems fundamentally different from the, let's say, "heroic" concept of Eisenstein's characters.*

AT: The vision of the world through the eyes of the hero is precisely what we wanted to achieve in our film. However, I'd like to add—in order to put an end to the problem of my relationship with Eisenstein—that I read in your press something that pleased me more than anything else, namely, that one could see that I was working without cutting myself off from traditions. I'd say more: I believe that nothing serious can be created without basing itself in tradition, for two reasons. The first is that you cannot withdraw from your Russian skin, from the links that you attach to your country, from the things you like, from what has previously been done in your country's cinema and in its art, and, therefore, from your native land. You cannot liberate yourself from all that. This is the main reason I consider myself traditional, a traditional director. The second reason is that the so-called "new" cinema while attempting to renew itself, tries, out of principle, to break away from traditions, and is essentially experimental. It aspires to be the starting point of the future of cinematic art. I don't believe that I have the right to experiment because I have a fundamentally serious attitude towards everything I do: I wish to obtain a result from the start. You can never attain a result from experimentation.

Eisenstein felt comfortable experimenting because, at the time, cinema was at its beginnings, and experimentation was the only possible path. Nowadays, given the established cinematic traditions, one shouldn't experiment anymore. At any rate, I myself wouldn't like to experiment. It takes up a lot of time and energy, and I consider that one has to be sure of what one is doing. An artist should no longer make rough drafts, should no longer try to draw vague sketches—he must create important films.

Finally, I would like to say that, if one absolutely needs to compare me to someone, it should be Dovzhenko. He was the first director for whom the problem of atmosphere was particularly important, and he loved his native land passionately. I share his love for my land, which is why I feel him very close to me. I'll add: he made his films as if they were vegetable gardens, as if they were gardens. He would water them himself, he would make everything grow with his own hands. . . . His love of the land and of the people made his characters grow, as it were, from the earth itself. They were organic, complete. I would very much like to resemble him in this respect. If I didn't succeed, I would feel mortified.

JS: *While watching* Roublev, *we felt that the real subject is the difficulty of being an artist, not only in the relationship to one's surroundings, but also in the search for oneself. For me, it is a film about the responsibilities and the destiny of the artist.*

AT: It's possible that that which you see as the main subject of the film may, indeed, be there. But that's more likely the result of the primary aim I'd set for myself while we were shooting this film. For us, it was important to demonstrate why we had chosen the character of Roublev, in essence an artist who is a genius. We were interested by the question: why is he a genius? And the result answered the questions you asked yourselves after watching the film. Not by accident does the character of Theophanes the Greek figure next to Roublev in the film. It is hard not to call him a genius because, in truth, he was a very great painter. However, when I think "Roublev" I say to myself "genius," whereas when I think of Theophanes, I don't know . . . I cannot say without hesitation that he is also a genius, because I have my own criterion of genius. My criterion consists of the following. An artist like Theophanes the Greek, indispensable in the film in order to bring out our conceptions, reflects the world. His work mirrors the world around him, his immediate reaction is to think that the world is put together badly, that man is perfidious and cruel, that he deserves to be punished even after his death, after the Last Judgement, if only because he is futile, depraved, and guilty: all of which is a normal reaction to the atmosphere of his time. When I'm afraid, this is how I react. I immediately condemn, if not the force that crushes me, the faults I attribute to men, to every man. There is a certain analogy with Kafka.

As for Roublev, he is opposed to Theophanes the Greek in the film. In what way? Roublev, like Theophanes, suffers from the hardships of his time, from the domestic battles prior to centralization, when the civil war doubled in intensity. He endured the incursions of the Tatar hordes and all the hardships that sprung up around him at the same time as Theophanes the Greek, but with a higher level of intensity. Theophanes the Greek could adopt a more remote, more philosophical attitude than Roublev because he was a painter covered with glory, he was not a monk, he was generally more cynical, he behaved like a foreigner, like a more experienced traveler from Byzantium. His point of view about life benefitted from an aloofness of which Roublev was incapable. In spite of seeing and perceiving this universe with great pain, Roublev abstains from reacting like Theophanes. He goes further. He doesn't express the unbearable weight of his life, of the world around him. He looks for the grain of hope, of love, of faith among the people of his time. He expresses it, through his own conflict with reality, not in a direct, but in an allusive manner, and therein lies his genius. He looks for a moral ideal within himself, and thereby expresses the hope and aspirations of the people, born of their living conditions. He expresses the attraction towards unity, fraternity, love—everything the people lack yet which Roublev feels to be indispensable. This is how he foresees Russian unification, a certain progress, and the hope in the only future that can get people involved by opening perspectives for them. His character, his image, goes beyond face value. He's very complex, he suffers, and therein lies his nobility. He expresses the hope and moral ideal of an entire people, and not only the artist's subjective reactions to the world around him. This is what was important for us.

This is precisely why we contrasted Theophanes the Greek to Roublev, this is precisely why we made Roublev suffer the temptations that weigh down upon his destiny. For precisely this reason the end, for us, must be creation, the only way out for Roublev. The creative aspirations of an entire people, which are symbolized by the boy who

casts the bell. That was the important thing. The rest is the consequence of what I tried to explain to you. Andrei Roublev was obviously
a man who was able to express himself, to express his ideal, and his
genius is to have made that ideal coincide with that of his people.
Whereas Theophanes the Greek is one who, like they say in the Orient,
"sings what he sees."

LS: *It seems to me that you also wanted to say that there is no master in*
art, that art cannot be taught, something one senses most clearly at the
end of the film.

AT: In a way, your observation is correct. But that is secondary, because
the essential thing for us was to say that experience is irreversible, that
every man has his own experience. And I don't believe that someone
could avoid taking his own experience into account. Individual experience is acquired with pain, with effort, with a degree of suffering. Only
after having been impregnated by these difficulties can experience bear
fruit. Your interpretation of the film in the sense that art cannot be
taught is only the explanation of a symbol. The important thing for us
was to show that experience is irreversible. For the story of Roublev, an
ideal character who was able to maintain his idea of morality, his love
of the people and his faith in the future, culminates at the moment of
his victory, a victory that is the result of his sufferings. Along with his
people, he was able to go through all the difficulties which, finally,
forced him to believe in that which he believed from the beginning.
However, in the beginning his belief was purely intellectual. It was the
ideal he had been taught in the monastery, the teachings of Sergei
Radonejsky, founder and ideologist of the monastery of the Trinity and
of Saint Serge. Roublev came out of it equipped with this science, but
without knowing how to use it. In real life, everything was different,
everything was upside down. Towards the end he believed more in this
ideal, the ideal of love and of the brotherhood between men, only
because he had been able to suffer for this ideal, alongside his people.
And from that moment on—which is the end of our film—his ideal
becomes unshakable for him, nothing can tear him away from it. In
fact, this idea finds its symbol in the boy who, in the last scene, says
that nobody taught him anything and that he had been forced to do
everything by himself. In this scene the boy is, in a way, Roublev's

double as far as ideas are concerned. He expresses the conclusion, the result of Roublev's life.

MC: *How do you explain the passage from black and white to color at the end of the film?*
AT: The appearance of color at the end of a black and white film allowed us to establish a connection, a relationship between two different notions. Here is what we wanted to say: black and white cinema is the most realistic because, according to me, color cinema has not yet attained the stage of realism. It still resembles photography and is, in all cases, exotic. Physiologically, man is incapable of being struck by color in life unless he is a painter, unless he voluntarily looks for the relationship between colors, unless he is particularly attracted to color. It so happens that the important thing for us was to talk about life. For me, life is translated in cinema by images in black and white. Even more so since we had to show a rapport between art, painting, on one hand, and life on the other. The association of the color finale and the black and white film expressed, for us, the relationship between Roublev's art and his life. In broad strokes it can be summed up in the following manner: on the one hand everyday, realistic, rational life, on the other the convention of the artistic expression of this life. We enlarged some details because it is impossible to translate painting, with its own dynamic and static laws, into cinema. We thereby made the spectator see in short sentences that which he would have seen had he contemplated Andrei Roublev's icons for hours on end. No analogies were possible there. It was only in the presentation of *details* that we tried to create the impression of the *whole* of his painting.

On the other hand, through a succession of details, we had the intention of leading the spectator toward a view of the entirety of *The Trinity*, the high point of Roublev's career. To bring the spectator towards this accomplished work by means of a sort of colored dramaturgy, making him wander through fragments towards a whole by creating a sort of flow of impressions. Third, this color ending, roughly 820 feet of film, was indispensable, as far as we were concerned, in order to make the spectator rest from the spectacle of the film, in order to prevent him from leaving the room right after the last black and white images, so he could have some time to detach himself from Roublev's life. We imposed time to think, in order to enable some ideas about the entire film to cross his mind while looking at the color and listening to the music so that, retrospectively, he would be able to imprint within himself some of the most important moments of the story. In a word, in order to prevent him from closing the book right away. I believe that, if the film had ended right after the "Bell" chapter, it would have been a failure. We absolutely had to hold the spectator in the screening room. This is the purely dramaturgical function of this last color scene. We also needed to give a continuation to the story of Roublev's life, in order to make people think about the fact that he was a painter, that this was what he painted, that he had put up with what he went through in order for it to express itself in certain colors. We felt the need to suggest all these thoughts to the spectator.

I would like to add this: the film ends with the image of the horses in the rain. In this manner, we wanted to come back to the symbol of life, because for me the horse symbolizes life. This may be my internal subjective vision, but the fact is that, when I see a horse, it seems to me that I have life itself before me. Because it is at the same time very beautiful, very familiar, and very significant in Russian life. In fact, there are a lot of horses in our film. An example: in the balloon sequence, there is a horse, and it is the horse who looks sad because of the death of the man who flew. Another horse dies during the sack of Vladimir and symbolizes all the horror of violence. In a manner of speaking, the horse is the witness and the symbol of life throughout the film. By returning to the image of the horses in the last shots, we wanted to highlight that the source of all of Roublev's art is life itself.

LS: *Is the absence of the sky in your film intentional? We never see the sky, only the earth. There isn't even any wind . . .*
AT: This is completely unconscious. What interests me at all times, and most of all, is precisely the earth. I am captivated by the process of growth of everything that comes from or grows on the earth: the trees, the grass . . . and all that stretches out toward the sky. Which is why in our film the sky only figures as the space towards which all that is born and that grows on the earth rises up. For me, the sky itself doesn't have a symbolic sense in and of itself. For me, the sky is empty. I'm only

interested by, I only give any importance to, its reflections on earth, in the river, in the puddles. When, in the film's first scene, the man flies, we only see the reflection of the sky on the earth, and that was our visual solution, out of principle. The relationship of the flying man with the earth was all that mattered, there was no relationship between him and the sky. In my opinion, directing is also a way to make events grow, just as in documentary films one can see plant stalks grow upward from the earth, visibly grow—images I am able to watch for hours on end. It's the same thing with the mise-en-scene. . . . I love the earth in general. I never see the mud, I only see the earth mixed with water, the mire from which things grow. I love the earth, I love *my* earth.

MC: *I have the feeling that there are pictorial inspirations in certain scenes, in their plastic conception, particularly in the Crucifixion seen from afar, as in a Brueghel painting. Have you really been inspired, or is it a coincidence?*

AT: It's true for this episode. It has, indeed, been inspired by Brueghel, whose work I like a lot. If we chose it, my cameraman and I, it's because Brueghel is close to Russians and makes a lot of sense for them. In the layering of levels, in the parallel action which exists in his paintings, in the numerous characters, each caught up in his own activities, there is something very Russian. If Brueghel's manner did not resonate with the Russian soul, we would never have used it in our film—it simply would not have crossed our minds. . . . In fact, I consider it a shortcoming of this scene, because the way we shot it, it incites the intellectual specta- tor to make this analogy, which is finally useless.

MC: *How did you get the idea to start your film with the scene of the flying man, a scene which surprised everyone?*

AT: It was for us the symbol of daring, in the sense that creation requires from man the complete offering of his being. Whether one wishes to fly before it has become possible, or cast a bell without having learned how to do it, or paint an icon—all these acts demand that, for the price of his creation, man should die, dissolve himself in his work, give himself entirely. That is the meaning of the prologue—the man flew, and for that he sacrificed his life.

MC: *What was the nature of your collaboration with Konchalovsky during the writing of the screenplay?*

AT: We started out talking, and we agreed on the general concept of the work. Then we looked for the film's structure. It was obvious that it should be made up of a succession of "short stories." We wanted to present a huge cross-section of life. We therefore determined the number of short stories to write in order to make up the film. For us, these stories are of equal importance. The general impression of the film is given by the contrast between the stories, or by the interference between their subjects and their plastic solution. After that . . . well, after that we would write. We talked in great detail about the content, the dialogues, the situation, and one of us, whichever one, it didn't matter, we wrote alternately—wrote the first draft. The one who wrote it handed it to the other, who added precise elements, and the back and forth operation would be repeated several times. Overtime we got so used to this system that we worked together—one of us would dictate to the other, who would type the text. In the end, the work process flowed from the thought process, which followed its course without any obstacle, in perfect understanding between the two authors.

LS: *Why was the first prologue, which figures in the original screenplay (in place of the flying man who, in the text, opened the second part of the film), and which was called "The battle in Koulikovo's field," not present in the film?*

AT: I did away with this scene because it was very expensive to shoot and the studio couldn't afford it.

LS: *There are numerous scenes of violence in your film, some of which seemed almost unbearable to me. In fact, in the exhibition Art of Ancient Russia, which is currently taking place at the Manège, I recognized one of your shots in the icon of Saint George. What are the reasons for this display of violence?*

AT: There are two reasons. The first is that, if you study what is said by any historian about those times, you will see that every page of Russian history preceding the centralization literally oozes blood. Literally! We reconstituted it in such a minimal measure that we sometimes felt that we were betraying historical truth. Afterwards we understood that it suffices to see all this blood appear on the screen, even in a feeble quantity, in order not to have to go any further. So this is the first reason: to be historically accurate. Second, the horrors that Andrei Roublev sees are indispensable to our subject matter. In so far as our narrative is very realistic, we could not limit Roublev's sufferings to the moral level, and only show the spiritual reflection of the trials he underwent: that would have taken us elsewhere, stylistically. Third, as a director, I always count on the effect shock produces on the spectator: no evasions, no long explanations about the horrors of war, because a short naturalistic scene suffices to put the spectator in a traumatic state, after which he will absolutely believe everything we show him.

I consider cinema to be a realistic art, and there is no reason to fear the increasing influence it has on the spectator. On the other hand, it seems to me that "literature," in the pejorative sense of the term, the principles of theatricality, weigh too heavily upon cinema and force it to avoid the realistic mode of expression. However, the good Lord himself wanted cinema to do only that! These are my three reasons . . .

MC: *How did you recruit your actors? Were they well-known or did you have other criteria?*
AT: The lead had to be someone nobody had ever seen in a film. For the part of Roublev, who everyone imagines in their own way, we could not insert someone who would evoke, by association, the image of other characters interpreted by him previously. Which is why we chose this little actor from the Sverdlosk theater who had only played small parts. In fact, after having read our screenplay, published in the *Iskusstvo Kino* magazine, he looked us up at Mosfilm, paying his own way, and he told us that nobody but he could play the part of Roublev. Indeed, after having done tests, we were convinced that only he would be suitable for the part.

We selected the other actors based upon our aversion to theatricality. I divide my actors into two categories: those who play a scene dramaturgically established by the screenplay, and those whose acting embodies the soul of the character, meaning, in a manner of speaking, parts that haven't been written because they are impossible to write. Some of these are Roublev himself; the mentally retarded woman played by my wife; Danila the Negro, whom we see in the first part of the film, played by Grinko; and finally Khan, interpreted by Bolot Bechenaleev, who played

The First Master in Konchalovsky's film. These are my favorite characters because they haven't been conceived dramaturgically, but were created by the actors, by their moods, by the milieu from which they stem.

MC: *Could you tell me which scenes were cut from the film?*
AT: First of all, nobody ever cut anything from my film. I'm the one who made cuts. The film's first version was three hours and twenty minutes long. The second, three hours fifteen. The last version was reduced by me to three hours and six minutes. I declare, and I insist on this point—it's my very sincere opinion—that the last version is the best one, the most accomplished, the "good" one according to me. As a matter of fact I only cut out places that were too long, and that the spectator doesn't even notice. These cuts don't change anything as regards subject matter, nor to the things we wanted to accentuate, nor to any important dialogues. In one word, we changed the timing, which had been badly calculated in the beginning. We did shorten some scenes containing violence, in order to create a psychological shock instead of a painful impression which would have gone against our aims. And all my comrades and fellow filmmakers who, during lengthy discussions, would advise me to make these cuts, were right. It took me a long time to recognize it. I imagined that they were putting pressure on my creative individuality, but afterwards I recognized that what was left over of the film was more than enough to accomplish the purpose I had set for my work. And I do not regret in the least to have brought the film down to its present length and state.

LS: *People have reproached you for the fact that you showed beautiful and joyful Mongolians in contrast to destitute and depressed Russians. What was your intention?*
AT: For me, it was important to give an exact idea of the Tatar yoke. This is how that translated: the Tatars were so sure of their strength—their domination lasted more than three centuries—that they behaved as if they were the masters of this land. And that is what was terrible for the Russians. When people told me about the last world war, the most frightening thing was to see the Germans walk around serenely, without any fear, along the Russian roads. Their calm attitude, their banal behavior was the most frightening.

And the crisis of the Tatar domination, which announced itself in 1380, after the battle in the field of Koulikovo, consisted in the forfeiture of an entire institution of slavery. During three hundred years the Tatars had very systematically plundered Russia. They had devised a system that allowed Russians to reconstitute their possessions between two Mongolian invasions, so that they could better profit from the pillages and the sacks. The beauty of the Tatars in the film is meant to express their calm assurance, their confidence in their supremacy. And that's where the situation of the Russians was tragic, those whose mission was to put up a barrier against the successive waves of Barbarians; a barrier that was fragile but indispensable to the safeguard of Western civilization. On the other hand, I don't believe that one has the right to humiliate the enemy by portraying him as physically ugly. Rather, we should show the moral superiority of those who fight against him.

MC: *What films do you like? Whose films do you like?*
AT: While doing *Roublev* I forced myself to be very hard and very dry, tending towards a sort of olympic calm that, for me, is the major quality of the art of directing a film. So I might as well tell you that I'm very fond of Bresson. But the person I like most is Dovzhenko. It seems to me that, if he had lived longer, he could still have made many interesting things. There are several directors I like, but their place changes according to the moment: Dovzhenko, Buñuel, Kurosawa, Antonioni, Bergman, and that's all. And of course Vigo, because he is the father of contemporary French cinema. It is even irritating to see to what extent he is plundered; however, up to now they haven't yet been able to steal all his possessions.

MC: *And among the young Soviet filmmakers?*
AT: I like Khutsiev a lot, he has great possibilities. He's preparing a film about Pushkin. I like certain aspects of Alov and Noumov a lot. Are you asking about the younger ones? You must understand that for me, in film, what counts is not the potential, but the result. Which is why it is very difficult for me to answer you. Our young directors are so young that they haven't yet been able to make their best films. As for guessing and talking about the future . . . I'm not a film critic, I don't know how to do that.

CIMENT, SCHNITZER, AND SCHNITZER/1969

LS: *Is there a relationship between Roublev and the screenplay you have just finished?*

AT: It's a strange thing. Every film I have directed and I intend to direct is always tied to characters who have something to overcome, who must succeed, in the name of this optimism on which I insist and which I constantly speak about. In other words, a man held up by an idea searches passionately for the answer to a question and goes to the end of his understanding of reality. And he reaches an understanding of that reality thanks to his experience.

Dialogue with Andrei Tarkovsky about Science-Fiction on the Screen

NAUM ABRAMOV/1970

ABRAMOV: *You're working on a film adaptation of the science-fiction novel* Solaris, *by Stanislaw Lem. Lately, the science-fiction genre has attracted the interest of many prominent filmmakers. This seems to be an indication of how the genre answers some sort of inner need for contemporary viewers and filmmakers alike. Complex, intellectual-artistic content can be combined in one film with aspects of a purely entertaining spectacle directed toward the widest possible audience. I think this is especially true for the genre of science-fiction in cinema. Viewers of different levels of sophistication would appreciate different elements of these films; in some cases the philosophical content, in other cases, the strictly superficial, dramatic, exciting aspects of the plot.*

In your opinion, what needs are satisfied in our time by the genre of science-fiction in cinema? Is it a desire to see the scientific and technological progress of humanity, incarnated in the vivid imagery of a contemporary film? Is it the expression of philosophical thought within the strange and thrilling context of a flight into space; the future of our planet; or the story of some brave, new invention? Maybe it's the striving of the writer and filmmaker to study people's character, our contemporary character, with the dramatic events dictated by the genre?

And finally, why have you turned to science-fiction, a genre which is so new to you?

TARKOVSKY: The questions you're asking, as far as I understand, are connected on one hand with filmmaking and on the other hand with

---

From *Ekran*, 1970–1971, 162–65. Translated from Russian by Jake Mahaffy and Yulia Mahaffy.

the viewer. But first, I want to explain why I decided to adapt Lem's novel, *Solaris*. Whether or not my first two films are good or bad, they are, in the final analysis, both about the same thing. They are about the extreme manifestation of loyalty to a moral debt, the struggle for it, and faith in it—even to the extent of a personality crisis. They are about an individual armed with conviction, an individual with a sense of personal destiny, for whom catastrophe is an unbroken human soul.

I'm interested in a hero that goes on to the end despite everything. Because only such a person can claim victory. The dramatic form of my films is a token of my desire to express the struggle and the greatness of the human spirit. I think you can easily connect this concept with my previous films. Both Ivan and Andrei do everything against their own safety. The first physically, the second in a spiritual sense. Both of them in a search for an ideal, moral way of living.

As for *Solaris*, my decision to adapt it to the screen is not at all a result of some fondness for the genre. The main thing is that in *Solaris*, Lem presents a problem that is close to me: the problem of overcoming, of convictions, of moral transformation on the path of struggle within the limits of one's own destiny. The depth and meaning of Lem's novel are not at all dependent on the science-fiction genre, and it's not enough to appreciate his novel simply for the genre.

The novel is not only about the human mind encountering the unknown, but it is also about the moral leap of a human being in relation to new discoveries in scientific knowledge. And overcoming the obstacles on this path leads to the painful birth of a new morality. This is the "price of progress" that Kelvin pays in *Solaris*. And Kelvin's price is the face to face encounter with the materialization of his own conscience. But Kelvin doesn't betray his moral position. Because betrayal in this situation means to remain at the former level, not even attempting to rise to a higher moral level. And Kelvin pays a tragic price for this step forward. The science-fiction genre creates the necessary premise for this connection between moral problems and the physiology of the human mind.

ABRAMOV: *And nevertheless, even though you emphasize your indifference to the genre, you are resolving this philosophical problem which concerns you within the genre of science-fiction. It seems to me that science-fiction creates such special conditions of cinematic representation for itself that it's impossible just to shrug them off. The filmmaker encounters different intellectual and artistic capacities in a novel and a film. He deals with the cinematic incarnation on screen of what was created by the imagination of the author of a literary work, with the need to provide the fantastic with a plastic specificity. These questions must have presented themselves to you.*

TARKOVSKY: The complexity in adapting *Solaris* is an issue of film adaptations in general and secondarily an issue of science-fiction adaptations. These are the two fundamental issues of my current work. The first issue relates to the principles of a work of literature in general. Prose possesses the special characteristic that its imagery depends on the sensory experience of the reader. So, no matter how detailed this or that scene is developed, the reader, to the degree of his own experience, sees that which his own experience, character, bias, and tastes have prepared him to see. Even the most detailed descriptions in prose, in a way, will elude the control of the writer and the reader will perceive them subjectively.

In the literal, superficial sense, *War and Peace* is read and envisioned by thousands of readers; this makes it a thousand different books as a result of the differences in experience between the writer and the reader. In this significantly important aspect is the special relevance and ubiquity of literature—its democracy, if you will. In this is the guarantee of the reader's co-creation. A writer subconsciously depends on an imaginative reader to see more and to see more clearly than the presented, laconic description. A reader can perceive even the most ruthless, naturalistic details with omission through his subjective, aesthetic filter. I would call this peculiarity of prosaic description to influence the reader "aesthetic adaptation." Principally, it governs perception and the prose author invades the soul of the reader within the belly of this Trojan horse.

This is in literature. But what about cinema? Where in cinema does a viewer have this freedom of choice? Each and every frame, every scene and episode, outwardly doesn't even describe, but literally records actions, landscapes, character's faces. And in this is the terrifying danger of not being accepted by the viewer. Because on film there is a very unambiguous designation of the concrete, against which the viewer's personal, sensory experience rebels.

Some may argue that cinema is attractive because it's really a source of what is exotic and unusual for a viewer. That isn't quite right. Actually, it's just the opposite. Cinema, in contrast to literature, is the filmmaker's experience caught on film. And if this personal experience is really sincerely expressed then the viewer accepts the film.

I've noticed, from my own experience, if the external, emotional construction of images in a film are based on the filmmaker's own memory, on the kinship of one's personal experience with the fabric of the film, then the film will have the power to affect those who see it. If the director follows only the superficial, literal base of the film, for example the screenplay, even if in the most convincing, realistic, and conscientious manner, the viewer will be left unaffected.

Therefore, if you're objectively incapable of influencing a viewer with his own experience, as in literature as I mentioned earlier, and you're unable to achieve that in principle, then in cinema, you should sincerely tell about your own experience. That's why even now, when all half-literate people have learned to make movies, cinema remains an art form, which only a small number of directors have actually mastered, and they can be counted with the fingers of one hand. To remold a literary work into the frames of a film means to tell your version of the literary source, filtering it through yourself.

ABRAMOV: *Where do you draw the line between a filmmaker's interpretation and the original work? Isn't there a danger of remolding the literary work to the point of losing its original stylistics and visual structure?*
TARKOVSKY: Working in science-fiction demands great subtlety and sincerity, especially if you're talking about the issue of perspective. That's why Lem is such a great science-fiction writer. You would understand what I mean if you read *Solaris*, *Eden*, and *Return from the Stars*.

In *Eden*, Lem tells about an expedition to a planet where the members of the expedition encounter a reality, the developmental laws of which they cannot comprehend. These laws slip away from understanding, like thoughts just forgotten. The air is filled with guesses and analogies, seen by the naked eye, but they can't be caught. It's a very specific, unnerving, and frustrating condition. And Lem does a brilliant job of expressing this condition. He describes in detail everything that the expedition encounters. But more than the detail, he describes what it is the people see, while not understanding what it means.

The same thing is in *Return from the Stars*. The protagonist returns from a flight to different galaxies. On earth, because of the differences in time (he has traveled at the speed of light), life has progressed through several generations. The returned astronaut walks through the city and doesn't understand anything. Lem describes everything the astronaut encounters in extreme detail and despite this detailed description, we don't understand anything either, along with the protagonist. These emotionally tense pieces express, for me, the quintessence of the author's personal experience projected into the future.

ABRAMOV: *The majority of directors of science-fiction movies think it necessary to impress the viewer's imagination with the concrete details of everyday life on other worlds or the details of a spacecraft's construction, which often crowd out the central idea of the film. I think Kubrick's* Space Odyssey *is guilty of that.*

TARKOVSKY: For some reason, in all the science-fiction films I've seen, the filmmakers force the viewer to examine the details of the material structure of the future. More than that, sometimes, like Kubrick, they call their own films premonitions. It's unbelievable! Let alone that *2001: A Space Odyssey* is phony on many points even for specialists. For a true work of art, the fake must be eliminated. I would like to shoot *Solaris* in a way that the viewer would be unaware of any exoticism. Of course, I'm referring to the exoticism of technology.

For example, if one shoots a scene of passengers boarding a trolley, which, let's say, we'd never seen before or known anything about, then we'd get something like Kubrick's moon-landing scene. On the other hand, if one were to shoot a moon landing like a common trolley stop in a modern film, then everything would be as it should. That means to create psychologically, not an exotic but a real, everyday environment that would be conveyed to the viewer through the perception of the film's characters. That's why a detailed "examination" of the technological processes of the future transforms the emotional foundation of a film, as a work of art, into a lifeless schema with only pretensions to truth.

Design is design. Painting is painting. And a film is a film. One should "separate the firmament from the waters" and not engage in making comic books.

When cinema moves out from under the power of money, namely, the costs of production, when there will be a method for the author of a work of art to record reality as with a pen and paper, paints and canvas, chisel and marble, "X" and the filmmaker, then we'll see. Then cinema will be the foremost art and its muse the queen of all the others.

I Love Dovzhenko

GÜNTER NETZEBAND / 1973

Q: *Andrei Tarkovsky, you are now forty-one years old. Your father is a famous poet. You devoted your attention to music and painting before film. Why did you choose film?*

T: That is difficult to say. It was purely coincidental. To answer this question more precisely: It seems to me that film deals with real forms, and operates with them. That is to say forms taken from real life. The occupation of film director reminds me in its essence of the act of creation, which is linked to the birth of new life, with a life that will happen upon the screen. The profession of director demands moral responsibility for the creation, a responsibility which we feel regarding our own behavior in our own life. It is to be sure a feeling of a special type of responsibility, and, to me, this work appeared extraordinarily interesting.

Q: *Could you comment on the stages of your life?*

T: In 1939, while I was still in elementary school, I also attended music school, in fact, piano class. Then the war began. I was forced to give up music school. My parents moved my sister and me closer to the Volga river. Two years later we returned to Moscow and I was able to continue my studies at the music school. I graduated from music school, although it was very difficult for my mother to provide for us—since famine prevailed. My mother paid for my music lessons through

From *Filmwissenschaftliche Beitraege Hochschule fuer Film und Fernsehen der DDR Sektion*, no. 14 (1973): 276–83. Reprinted by permission. Translated from German by Karin Kolb.

enormous self-sacrifice. And then I started to take up painting. But I became neither a musician nor a painter, although I have to say that I regret very much that I gave up music. This was one of the serious mistakes I made in my life.

Q: *Why?*

T: Because in my opinion music is the highest form of art, notwithstanding the fact that music is received on an emotional level and presents pure abstraction. That means that music is most vividly and most profoundly able to express the idea of creation. I do not regret that I did not become a painter. After I attended both schools I took up Asian studies. Soon enough, after two years, I realized that I would "die" there. That was not at all my cup of tea. After I had given up Asian studies I went to Siberia, where I worked at a geological research station as a collector for two years. It was a fantastic time. In 1954, I was accepted at the Moscow Film Institute. Mikhail Romm was my teacher. I defended my diploma in 1960, and my thesis received first prize. Those would be the most important facts. You know the rest of my biography . . .

Q: *There are a lot of different interpretations of your movie* Andrei Roublev. *I think it is a multi-layered, multidimensional movie. There are opinions that the movie is not historically accurate, too long, too naturalistic, too gruesome. And you stated once that your opus should be seen with "modern eyes."*

T: The goal of the work was certainly not to simply reconstruct the life of Andrei Roublev. Our film is not a biographical film. And not only because there exist no details of his life, but also because we followed a different intention. We did not want to make a historical film. We wanted to show the interaction of the painter and the people whose will he was, after all, expressing. Evidently unconsciously. We wanted to communicate the meaning of creation. Frankly, it was important to us to prove that a painter of genius like Roublev was capable of sensing the longing and the quest of the nation he belonged to. We wanted to show that real creativity is always as follows: that a painter, up to the last iota, into all fibers of his heart, is burning with the flame of his creation. There are no circumstances where it is permissible to take away his right to create. Furthermore, the cruelty and darkness of that time, a time where brutality was reaching a pinnacle, still prompted us to portray Roublev in a way that showed that he aspired to the ideals he was portraying in his paintings. And these ideals are love, fraternity, and unification. Behind unification I perceive the reality of people striving to get in touch with one another since the history of that period was unfolding on the eve of such a process, a process in which people would find each other. And if there was criticism that my movie was too cruel, in my opinion this is sheer moralizing.

Were one to generalize about the aim of our movie, it is by all appearances the portrayal of a painter, an artist, who is unable to create if he is not an artist. The point here is not the idealistic position of someone with regard to his or her own thoughts. One might assume that Roublev was such a person, that he painted very delicately and in silence in his monk's cell, removed from the world. I cannot believe in such a Roublev. No one would believe in such a Roublev. That's what we wanted to make a film about. Essentially Roublev is a fighter. And his battlefield is the human spirit.

Q: *Would you agree with me in thinking that it is normal that a socialist artist also has to fight for the things he is doing? And the things he is convinced of?*
T: I have no doubt about that. He is born to fight anyway. Especially if you're talking about fighting for his own beliefs. It was for me very bitter to hear the accusations, that people believed I was a weak person unable to express the truth, the conviction of one's beliefs. On the other hand everyone who works creatively feels this state of struggle since he creates images in his mind even in the face of enormous, dreadful resistance. The artist is himself the cornerstone of all these impingements upon his creativity. It seems to me that the most horrid, the most irreconcilable struggle is the one with oneself. And therefore all the other struggles that date back a long time ago are simply episodes from a normal, natural life. I felt it was necessary for me to show my love, my tender feeling for the Russian culture, for Russian people, for the Russian soul, and for history in the Roublev film. One should not forget that over the centuries Russia always stood between the West and the "wild" East. It did not engage in what Europe engaged in at that time: the process of European Renaissance. At that time

Russia had to resist the Tatars. I wanted to depict the serious circumstances of that time. And I wanted to tell the story of a painter who, through the magnitude of his personality, was able to give back belief, hope, and love to his country. The love for his own people, the belief in their future. The art historians who have studied Roublev agree with that. And also—one should never make "sweet" movies that are the equivalent of relaxing in a soft chair. These are essentially Matisse's words. With this attitude I believe that I convey my deep respect for the millions of people who have watched my film or will watch my film.

Q: *I would now to like to talk about* Ivan's Childhood, *your debut feature film, and I quote Andrei Tarkovsky: "It is a typical work of youth. At that time I had no coherent, thought-out concept, I dealt with things in an elementary way." My question: is it really a mistake to shoot a first film "elementarily"?*

T: I do not know. I saw *Ivan's Childhood* again two years ago and it seemed to me to be a weak film in the sense that there are a lot of scenes where the author betrays his taste, and there are a lot of scenes where he needed to be stronger "emotionally." One should speak with one's own language. *Ivan's Childhood* is a film that bears the signature of a young man who does not quite know how to express himself and who has not yet found his own language.

Q: *Do you see a continuity and a relationship between the heroes of your films—Ivan, Roublev, the astronaut Kris in* Solaris? *If so, what is the character of this relationship?*

T: It is obvious that there is a connection between them, because all three characters in all three films are analyzed in a critical dilemma where either they die or abandon their beliefs. Or where they simply give up. It seems to me that the tendency to navigate the hero into a hopeless or into a dire situation where a man would inescapably be faced with making a choice is what brings all heroes nearer to one another. They speak on my behalf about how difficult it is for a human being. How difficult it is to be a human being. It would be easier sometimes to give up. It is by far more difficult to be faithful to one's beliefs. Ivan lets go of his childhood, he renounces his childhood to be able to fight against Fascism and he becomes an adult. Roublev not only finds strength but also meaning in his suffering and in this gains perspective on his behavior. Kris in *Solaris*, placed into un-human conditions, preserves his humanity. Because the people on this space station have only to solve one problem: how to remain human. And they are dealing with it in very different ways. It is surely of interest to probe the character of one's protagonists, even in such an unbelievable situation that demands such a big decision. All three simply do not let go of their belief. They stay faithful to themselves. They preserve their individuality–regardless of what will come. In this sense these three form one uniform whole.

Q: *You were a student of Mikhail Romm. What do you have to thank him for?*

T: First of all, that he accepted me into his class at the Moscow State Film Institute. He was the only one in favor of my studying at the Institute. The admission committee was against me. In my opinion, Mikhail Romm is one of the best teachers because he never tried to force his opinion upon us. He had the gift to see the ability of his students and to develop them further, and he respected personality the most, the feeling of one's own dignity, that not everyone is alike.

Q: *Which paragons of the Soviet film do you feel indebted to? Which filmmaker are you close to?*

T: For me this question has long ago been decided. I love Alexander Dovzhenko very much. I believe he is a genius. He created a film which I have not stopped watching over and over again to this day: that is *Earth*. I cannot explain why this film touches me so deeply. The film may be naïve in many ways, too schematic, rather roughly composed. But—the attention of this film is focused on the workingman who tills the land he lives on. And that surely is one of the noblest professions on earth. I probably did not express it accurately, I mean this profession ennobles people. I have lived a lot among very simple farmers and met extraordinary people. They spread calmness, had such tact, they conveyed a feeling of dignity and displayed wisdom that I have seldom come across on such a scale. Dovzhenko had obviously understood wherein the sense of life resides. And he addressed an issue that has left a lasting impression on me. This trespassing of the border between nature and mankind is an ideal place for the existence of man. Dovzhenko understood this. I think about him a lot—he forces me to think about him. Dovzhenko not only gives the impression of being a director. He is a philosopher.

Of course there are also contemporary film directors who mean a great deal to me. For example I think that Giorgi Shengelaya—he made *Pirosmani*—and Otar Iosseliani are extremely gifted. They will make a lot more wonderful films. I would, however, put Iosseliani with his two films, *Lived Once a Song-Thrush* and *When Leaves Fall*, before all others.

Q: *What is your conception of filmmaking in this present time of ideological class struggle? What do you think about Brecht's statements that one has to activate the joy of cognition and organize the fun of changing reality? And elsewhere he says: The illustration of the new is not easy, it is a question of enthusiasm for the new. The socialist-realist way of composition needs constant training, change, formation of something new. Above all it must be aggressive. And as a fighter, it needs all weapons, always better weapons . . .*

T: I agree entirely with this point of view. But I would add that in the life of every artist this form of fighting adopts a different nuance. In this conclusion of Brecht's, his attitude towards art is expressed. I share this point of view and I am of the opinion that art is a strong weapon. Sometimes art is even underestimated.

A few years ago I had the opportunity to get familiar with Bertolucci's first films. I had the impression that this young Italian director is a very talented, strong artist who has something to say. Now he has turned into a commercial director. In his latest film *Last Tango in Paris* (1972), Bertolucci could not stop himself from using pornography. He betrayed his whole talent just to show what impotent and esoteric people, a bourgeois audience, enjoy. Before, Bertolucci had appeared as someone who would fight for his political views. Now he has stopped being an artist. Nobody forced him to make this movie. He forgot that the art he creates is not his property. It belongs to people who respect the artist and his work. He is obviously missing the sense that with the freedom an artist has he also takes on responsibilities and duties. And one has to understand what that is—an artist. Because one has to permanently conquer it. And one is not allowed to trade with it.

The Artist Lives Off His Childhood like a Parasite: An Interview with the Author of *The Mirror*

CLAIRE DEVARRIEUX/1978

"I HAVE FEW THINGS to say about women," says Andrei Tarkovsky. "The subject of my film is a man who unites women and children. However, he is not accomplished as a son or a husband, and the children lack a man, a father. So, he's the storyteller, he stays off-screen. We only see him when he is six, and then when he is twelve, during the war.

"Relationships have been broken and the storyteller has to renew them, in order to find his moral equilibrium, but he is unable to do so. He lives with the hope that he will be able to pay his love debt back, but that debt is one which nobody can get rid of.

"Women can only destroy everything. No, no, I'm joking. We can understand their role in this way, but we love them, they brought us up, they made us the way we are. They are steadfast, they want to maintain the child in us, whereas we are already old men. *The Mirror* is not a casual title. The storyteller perceives his wife as the continuation of his mother, because wives resemble mothers, and errors repeat themselves—a strange reflection. Repetition is a law, experience does not get transmitted, everyone has to live it.

From *Le Monde*, 20 January 1978, 18. Reprinted by permission. Translated from French by Susana Rossberg.

"Nature is always present in my films, and it's not a question of style. It's the truth. While my father was fighting in the war, my mother would take us to the countryside every spring. She considered it her duty, and ever since then I associate nature with my mother.

"A city man knows nothing about life, he doesn't feel how time passes, he doesn't know its natural flow. The child finds assurance of its future in nature, in nature he educates his will. And the circumstance of being alone allows him to have the capacity to meet other people later on. If one is only a social animal, one survives, consigned to the wills of others. Unconsciously, my mother knew that nature is indispensable, and she instilled in us a peasant culture.

"My wife and I bought a little house out in the countryside a couple of years ago. I'm delighted to see my son's impatience to go there soon. And yet, he will be the only child there. My son's Russian side is linked to that family concept, to that respect of nature."

"After this film, I remember nothing. Memory is a gift of this minute, it's the state of the second in which I speak, and not a look towards the past. This past which I carry around on a shoulder-belt like a necessary but sometimes too heavy piece of baggage.

"All artistic work relies on memory, and is a means of crystallizing it. Like an insect on a tree, the artist lives off his childhood like a parasite. Afterwards, he spends what he has accumulated, he becomes an adult, and maturity is the end."

"In Paris, I have asked to meet Bresson. We have nothing in common, but he's one of the best directors I know. I want to see him, to see his face, to see how he talks. I have no questions to ask him, he himself suffices for me. I have always envied him because he doesn't get agitated over the 'client,' like we say back home. He uses very few means of expression, nobody has ever reached such a degree of asceticism.

"He looks for the possibility of talking about life, of showing its unique aspect, the non-repetition of every gesture on screen. But the contradiction is that each gesture is banal. He expresses that which is typical through that which is unique, and this ability to link the infinitely large to the infinitely small has always moved me. It seems to me that I have always understood what he was trying to say."

Interview with Andrei Tarkovsky

TONINO GUERRA / 1978

In Moscow, Tonino Guerra, Italian poet and screenwriter (he has worked with Petri, Rosi, Antonioni, and with Fellini on Amarcord*) met with Andrei Tarkovsky, the maker of* Andrei Roublev, *whose last film* The Mirror, *is finally being released in France.*

With respect to this nostalgic film about the persistence of our first memories, Tonino Guerra asked Tarkovsky about childhood, death, and the nature of dreams. It is expected that Tarkovsy will begin shooting a new film Italian Journey, *based on an idea by Tonino Guerra.*

G: *What is your earliest memory?*
T: The first thing that I remember happened when I was a year and a half. I remember the house, the open terrace, the stairs from the terrace—only five or six steps—and the railing. Between the staircase and the angle of the house was an enormous lilac bush. It was a cool and sandy place. I would roll an aluminum hoop from the gate to the lilacs. At one point I hear a strange noise coming from the sky. I am seized with a panicked fear of dying, and hide myself beneath the lilacs. I look up at the sky since that's where the noise is coming from. There's a fearsome noise that becomes more and more intense. All of a sudden, between the branches I see an airplane pass. It's 1933. I never thought it might be a bird, but something very terrible.

From *Télérama*, no. 1462 (January 21–27, 1978). Reprinted by permission. Translated from French by Deborah Theodore.

G: *How did your parents get along with each other?*
T: It's hard to talk about that. I was only three when my father left the family. Afterwards, we saw him but rarely. I'm left with two impressions. The first is this one: we lived in a small, two-room apartment in the old part of Moscow. My father, as you know, is a poet, and stayed up all night sometimes to write. He typed on a machine. I would hear him asking my mother every night, "Maruschka, tell me whether you like it better this way or that way," and he would read her a line. My father generally accepted her suggestions.

For the second memory, contrarily, I am a few years older; I have already started school. And my father came home very late one night. My sister and I were asleep already, and he started a fight with my mother in the kitchen. He wanted me to go to live with him in the other house. My mother didn't want it. That night I couldn't go back to sleep because I was asking myself what I should say the next day if they asked me who I wanted to live with. I realized that I would never go to live with my father, even though I missed not seeing him.

G: *How do you view death?*
T: I have no fear of death, really no fear. It does not frighten me. It is physical suffering that frightens me. Sometimes I think that death could give a surprising feeling of freedom. The kind of freedom that's often impossible in life. Therefore I do not fear death. What is very sad, on the other hand, is the death of a loved one.

Clearly, when we mourn the loss of those we hold dear it's because we realize that we will never again have the possibility of asking their forgiveness for all of our sins against them. We cry at their gravesides, not because we feel bad for them but because we feel bad for ourselves. Because we can no longer be forgiven.

G: *Do you believe that when a man dies everything is over, or that another kind of life continues?*
T: I am convinced that life is only the beginning. I know that I can't prove it, but instinctively we know that we are immortal. It's hard for me to explain because it's very complex. I just know that a man who ignores death is a bad man.

G: *Tell me what you want to do with your next film. I don't need the plot, just your point of departure, the idea that you like.*

T: I would like to film a scene against a window or a veranda with panes of glass that reflect the sun as it is setting. I already know that it takes five minutes for the sun to set. Then I would like the characters to speak their lines while the sun is setting so that very slowly the light in the windows will get dimmer and then go out. One moment the sun is there, and then five minutes later it is night.

I would also like to film the instant when the first snow begins to fall, the kind of snow that whitens the ground and dissolves in two minutes. All the while the characters are in action.

Often we remove nature from films because it seems useless. We exclude it thinking that we are the real protagonists. But we are not the protagonists, because we are dependent on nature. We are the result of its evolution. I think to neglect nature is, from an emotional and artistic point of view, a crime. Above all it is stupid, because nature always gives us the sensation of the truth.

G: *I know that you have a little dacha in the country and that you retreat to it from time to time.*

T: It's a log house about two hundred miles from Moscow. It's the first time I've ever owned my own home. This is how I came to have a relationship with animals . . . a cat, a dog . . . I probably owe the possibility of knowing animals at all entirely to my wife. Since she started living in the country birds fly around her, perch on her shoulder, on her head. Whatever it is, they never come near me but they walk alongside of Larissa.

G: *Do you give a lot of importance to dreams?*

T: There are two kinds of dreams. Those that you forget right away and the others that have a colossal importance. I would like to understand them deeply because they are messages.

G: *What is your most recent dream?*

T: Yesterday. One of my recurring dreams about war. War had just erupted. I seemed to be cold, marching with many others, stepping over bodies. We could only feel the bodies with our feet because we had

our eyes fixed on an enormous television screen where a big expert con-
soled us by saying that our scientists had succeeded in finding a way to
increase the rotation of the earth so that our rockets would fire faster
than the enemy's. And in fact we could feel the earth turning beneath
our feet as if we were bears on a giant ball, and there was this big TV
screen with a fine grainy powder on it like snow over the face of the
person speaking, and there was also snow on us and, very slowly, everything became a walk in the snow . . . almost a joyful moment. And
then I'm walking and I see only white.

Stalker, Smuggler of Happiness

TONINO GUERRA/1979

ACCORDING TO SOVIET AUTHORITIES, *Stalker*, Tarkovsky's last film, was not ready for the Cannes Festival. It's just as well for Andrei Mikhalkov Konchalovsky, who has just won the Special Jury Prize with *Siberiade*. It's too bad for Tarkovsky, the mystical poet of *Andrei Roublev* and *The Mirror*, whose fabulous images still haunt us.

TG: *What does "Stalker" mean?*
AT: It's a made-up word that comes from the English verb "to stalk": to approach furtively. In this film this word indicates the profession of one who crosses the borders and penetrates a forbidden Zone with a specific objective, a bit like a bootlegger or a smuggler. The Stalker's craft is passed on from one generation to the next. In my film, the forbidden Zone represents the places where desires can be satisfied.

The spectator may doubt its existence or see it merely as a myth or a joke . . . or even as the fantasy of our hero. For the viewer this remains a mystery. The existence in the Zone of a room where dreams come true serves solely as pretext to revealing the personalities of the three protagonists.

TG: *What kind of person is the Stalker?*
AT: He's a very honest man, clean, and intellectually innocent. His wife describes him as "cheerful." He leads men into the Zone to, he

From *Télérama*, no. 1535 (June 13, 1979). Reprinted by permission. Translated from French by Deborah Theodore.

says, make them happy. He gives himself completely to this task, with total lack of self-interest. He believes that it's the only way to make people happy. In the end his is the story of the last of the idealists. It's the story of a man who believes in the possibility of happiness independent of the will and the capacity of man. His job gives meaning to his life. As if he were a priest of the Zone, the Stalker leads men there to make them happy. In reality, no one can say for sure if anyone there is happy.

At the end of his journey in the Zone, under the influence of the people he is leading, he loses faith in the possibility of making all of mankind happy. He can no longer find anyone who believes in this Zone or in the happiness to be found in this room. In the end he finds himself alone with his idea of human happiness achieved by a pure faith.

TG: *When did the idea of this film come to you?*
AT: I had recommended a short novel, *Picnic on the Roadside*, to my friend, the filmmaker Giorgi Kalatozishvili, thinking he might adapt it to film. Afterwards, I don't know why, Giorgi could not obtain the rights from the authors of the novel, the Strugatsky brothers, and he abandoned the idea of this film. The idea began to turn in my head, at first from time to time and then more and more often. It seemed to me that this novel could be made into a film with a unity of location, time, and action. This classic unity—Aristotelian in my view—permits us to approach truly authentic filmmaking, which for me is not action film, outwardly dynamic.

I must say, too, that the script of *Stalker* has nothing in common with the novel, *Picnic on the Roadside*, except for the two words, "Stalker" and "Zone." So you see the history of the origins of my film is deceptive.

TG: *Do the images that you've shot suggest specific musical accompaniment?*
AT: When I saw the rushes for the first time, I thought the film wouldn't need any music. It seemed to me that it could—that it must even—rely solely on sounds. Now I would like to try muted music, barely audible, behind the noise of trains that pass beneath the windows of the Stalker's home. For instance, Beethoven's Ninth Symphony

("Ode to Joy"), Wagner, or even the Marseillaise. In any case, music that is more or less popular, that expresses the movement of the masses, the theme of humanity's social destiny.

But this music must be barely heard beneath the noise, in a way that the spectator is not aware of it. Moreover, I would like most of the noise and sound to be composed by a composer. In the film, for example, the three people undertake a long journey in a railway car. I'd like that the noise of the wheels on the rails not be the natural sound but elaborated upon by the composer with electronic music. At the same time, one mustn't be aware of music, nor of natural sounds.

TG: *But will there be a central theme?*
AT: I think the theme will be Far Eastern, a kind of Zen music, where the principle is concentration rather than description. The main musical theme will have to be, on the one hand, purged of all emotion, and on the other, of all thought or programmatic intent. It must express its truth about the world around us in an autonomous way. It must be self-contained.

TG: *Can you describe to me, image by image, the end of the film, as if I were blind?*
AT: It would probably be great not to make films, but instead to simply describe them to blind people. A wonderful idea! One would only need to buy a tape recorder. "Thought expressed is a lie," said the poet.

TG: *So, I can't see. Tell.*
AT: In the foreground, a sick little girl, Stalker's daughter. She holds a large book in front of her face. She is wearing a scarf. She is in profile against an illuminated window. Slowly, the camera pulls back and frames a part of the table. The table in the foreground with dirty dishes on it: two glasses and a teapot. The little girl puts the book down on her knees, and we hear her voice repeating what she has just read. She looks at one of the glasses. The glass, under the force of her look, moves towards the camera. The child looks at the other glass and the other glass also begins to move forward. And then the child looks at the glass at the edge of the table and it falls to the floor without breaking. We then hear a train passing very close by, making a strange sound. The

walls shake more and more. The camera goes back to the girl in the foreground and in the midst of this crashing noise the film ends.

TG: *Are you thinking about another film right away after* Stalker*?*
AT: I would like to make the film that we decided to make together: *Italian Journey.* But you can talk about that better than I can. I would like to make a film that would lose some viewers and gain others, new ones. I would like our film to be seen by different people than those we call film viewers.

TG: *I was told that you would like to change your style completely. Is this true?*
AT: Yes, only I don't know how yet . . . It would be great for me to make a film with the freedom of a beginner. To turn down big financing. To have the possibility to observe nature and men at my leisure, without haste. And the subject would emerge of itself, as the result of these observations and not necessarily planned down to the smallest detail.

Such a film would have to be made in complete freedom, independent of inspiration, of actors, of camera angles and shots. And with a discreet camera . . . It seems to me that making a film in this way would push me to go much further.

TG: *What images do you think you've "stolen" from someone else, even though you've obviously transformed them into your own style?*
AT: I'm generally very wary of this and I try to avoid it. I don't like the suggestion that I may not have acted in such or such a situation with complete independence. Yet, lately, these references begin to interest me. In *The Mirror* for instance, there are two or three shots that are very clearly inspired by Brueghel: the boy, the small silhouettes of men, the snow, the bare trees, and the river in the distance. I created these shots very consciously and deliberately, not with the idea of copying or to show culture but to bear witness to my love for Brueghel, of my dependence on him, of the deep impression that he has made on my life.

In *Andrei Roublev*, there was a scene that might have been from Mizoguchi, the great departed Japanese director. I wasn't aware of it until it was projected. It's the one where the Russian prince gallops across the countryside on a white horse, and the Tatar is on a black horse. The quality of the image in black and white, the landscape, the opacity of the overcast sky had a strange resemblance to an ink-drawn Chinese landscape.

The two riders gallop after each other. Suddenly the Tatar cries out, whistles, whips his horse, and overtakes the prince. The Russian goes after him but cannot catch up. In the next shot, they have stopped. There is nothing else. Just the memory of the Russian prince on his white horse trying to catch the Tatar and unable to do it.

It's a scene that has nothing to do with the plot of the story. It attempts to express the state of a soul and to throw light on the nature of the relationship between the two men. It's like a game that two boys play. One runs ahead and says, "You can't catch me!" The other one takes off after him running as fast he can, but he can't catch him. Then right afterwards, they forget their game and stop running.

Interview with Andrei Tarkovsky (on *Stalker*)

ALDO TASSONE/1980

Q: *In a forbidden forest–the Zone–there is a Room in which one's desires are fulfilled. . . . Watching* Stalker *in Cannes—just once, unfortunately, and during frequent blackouts, I thought of these lines: "Near jasmine is a stone; beneath that stone is a hidden treasure . . ."*

T: Those are the first words of "The White Day," a poem written by my father, Arseni. At first, the script for *The Mirror* was to be called *The White Day*, before it actually became what it is. But an epigraph is a collection of words, and you can't choose them in a logical way. The choice is always a little random. It's a whim, and you can use whatever you want as long as the words are beautiful.

Q: *Is the Room of Desire an invention of* Stalker? *Was it in the novel by the Strugatsky brothers upon which the film is based? What does it represent for you?*

T: In the original story by the Strugatsky brothers, which is very different from the script, there was a place where desires were fulfilled. But this was represented by a gold orb. There was a golden orb, for whatever reason. However, in the Strugatsky story, the desires were truly fulfilled, whereas in the script this remains a mystery. You don't know whether this is true or whether it's the Stalker's fantasy. For me as the author of the film, either choice is OK. It seems to me that it's just as well if it is all a part of his fantasy–that would not affect the main point at all. What's important is that the two travelers don't enter the room.

From *Positif*, no. 247 (October 1981). Reprinted by permission. Interview took place in Rome in July, 1980. Translated from French by Vasiliki Katsarou.

Q: *And why don't they enter the room?*

T: Well, for one thing, the Stalker doesn't enter because it wouldn't be right for him to enter. He doesn't have to. It goes against his beliefs. Furthermore, if it's all in his imagination, then he doesn't go in because he knows his desires won't be fulfilled there. For him, the important thing is that the two others believe the Room can fulfill their desires, and that they enter. Even if in fact nothing happens. The Stalker needs to find people who believe in something, in a world that no longer believes in anything. Now, why doesn't the Writer enter? We don't know, and neither does he. He knows neither where he's going nor what he's looking for. We know he's a talented person, but already used up, and what he's writing now is what he's expected to write by critics, publishers, and the public. He's simply a popular author. And he no longer wants to continue down that road. At first, it seems to him that if he enters the Room, he'll be able to write better. He'll become the person he was when he first started writing, and he'll be able to rid himself of whatever has been weighing him down. But afterwards, his thinking changes and he asks himself: if I change, if my inspiration is restored, why would I continue to write since I would already know that whatever I would write would be automatically genius? The point of writing is to surpass oneself, to show others what one can do, that one can do even better. If someone already knows himself to be a genius, why write at all? What remains to be proven? Creation is a manifestation of one's will.

If the artist is a genius from the outset, his art loses all meaning. Furthermore, the Writer considers the story of "Porcupine," who was the Stalker's teacher, and who hung himself. He concludes that in that Room it isn't one's desires that are fulfilled but rather a hidden vision lying deep within the heart of each person. These are true desires, which correspond to one's interior world. For instance, if it's wealth that I crave, that probably won't be what I receive, but rather something closer to the truth of my heart—poverty, for example, which is what my soul truly clamors for. These are hidden desires. The Writer is afraid of entering the Room because he has a pretty low opinion of himself.

As for the Scientist, he doesn't want to enter at all. From the beginning. In fact, he is carrying a bomb to blow it up. That's because for him, the Room is a place that disturbed people could visit and thereby endanger all of life on earth. But he abandons his plan because it's not reasonable to fear that people motivated by a desire for total power would come to the Room. Also because in general people are motivated by things that are extremely basic like money, status, sex . . . That's why he doesn't destroy the Room. The other reason is that the Stalker convinces him not to do it, by telling him that such a place needs to be saved. Where people can come and still hope, people who want something, who need an ideal.

Q: *In the end, the Stalker bemoans the cowardice of these men who won't enter the Room. He wonders about their attitude.*
T: Obviously, they didn't enter because they are afraid. First of all, the Writer is afraid. He has a highly developed sense of his own insignificance and at the same time he figures: why should I go in if nothing is going to happen in there anyway? On the one hand, he understands that desires can't be fulfilled and that they won't be fulfilled there. And on the other hand, he's afraid. It's a very contradictory and superstitious position. That's why the Stalker is so upset. Because no one truly believes in the existence of the Room.

The Writer definitely denies its existence. He says, "It probably doesn't exist at all," and asks the Professor, "Who told you that it exists?" The Scientist points to the Stalker. It's he who is the only witness to the existence of the Room, the only one who has faith. All information about it comes from him, so it's easy to imagine that he made it all up. For him, what's worse is not that they were afraid but that they didn't believe. That faith no longer has any place in the world.

Q: *What sort of faith are you referring to?*
T: Faith is faith. Without it, man is deprived of any spiritual roots. He is like a blind man. Over time, faith has been given different content. But in this period of the destruction of faith, what's important to the Stalker is to light a spark, a belief in the heart of people.

Q: *Access to the Zone is forbidden by the authorities. Is this a metaphor? Does this mean that the powers that be do not want people to achieve their true desires?*
T: It's difficult for me to say why it's forbidden. It could be for any reason. It's true that it would be very dangerous to let people enter the

Zone, since they could enter with desires that are very dangerous for society at large. It's probably the instinct for self-preservation. It's natural, and furthermore every society has an interest in maintaining its own stability.

Q: *The paths leading to the Room are constantly changing. It's hard to know which to choose. Danger could lurk anywhere.*
T: The trip's security is dependent on the interior makeup of each individual, as the Stalker makes known in one of his speeches. If travelers come with sincere desires, they have nothing to fear. Otherwise, everything changes and the place becomes dangerous. Obstacles may spring up, changes . . .

Q: *The piece of cloth anchored by a metal bolt is a striking visual image . . .*
T: It has no particular meaning. How can you decide if the path is dangerous or not, not knowing what is ahead? But this, you can throw far ahead.

Q: *At a certain point, one of them is separated from the others, and then he mysteriously catches up with them at the same place where he left them, as if in a dream . . .*
T: It's the Scientist who moves away because he's looking for his backpack. Why do they find him in the same place? First of all, they could have gotten lost. That's one answer. Furthermore, if the Zone has the powers that the Stalker say it does, then there could be a million explanations for this phenomenon. Finally, it's conceivable that he is leading them on these detours on purpose in order to create a magical atmosphere. You can never know for sure whether the Room exists or not. That's the whole problem.

Q: *And the phone ringing in the derelict house? It's a beautiful image, but how can that happen?*
T: Well, after all, it's very possible that an old telephone could be there, that it wasn't destroyed and that someone is on the line . . . Why is that impossible?

Q: *The Stalker is something of a prophet. He's a Christ-like figure . . .*
T: Yes, he's a prophet who believes that humanity will perish for lack of a spiritual life. Actually, this story is about the crisis of one of the world's last remaining idealists.

Q: *Why is the film called* Stalker, *and not* The Room of Desires *or quite simply,* The Zone?
T: *The Room of Desires* is too banal. I'd like to think that the film is realistic, and not fantasy or science-fiction. *The Zone* has an overly specific, technological meaning. Whereas *Stalker* is the name of the person telling the story, quite simply. It's his story that's important.

Q: *How do you see the end of your film?*
T: They go back. His wife sees that he has broken down completely, because no one believes it, believes his story.

Q: *And the little girl?*
T: His wife finally asks him, "Do you want me to go with you?" and he answers, "No one will ever go with me again, because no one hopes for anything any more." She insists, "Do you want me to go with you, because I too have something I want?" He answers, "No, you shouldn't go, because you might waver as well." This is not very understandable. He refuses to take her for reasons we don't really understand. Maybe because the Writer convinced him that nothing could ever happen there again, that the place is unhealthy and useless. That may be why he shouldn't bring his wife there. But he should bring others there in order to pass on this virus of idealism. I don't know about the little girl . . . She represents hope, quite simply. Children are always something hopeful. Probably because they are the future. In any case, that's the way life is.

Q: *And the little girl's mysterious powers?*
T: From a symbolic point of view, they represent new perspectives, new spiritual powers that are as yet unknown to us, as well as new physical forces. Furthermore, they could represent something else. People have always looked forward to the end of time as we know it, probably because their lives didn't satisfy them. Despite this, life goes

on. It's true that today we have a nuclear bomb and this contributes to the apocalyptic dimension.

Q: *Who will Stalker travel with next time?*
T: I had this idea to make another film whose main characters would be the wife, the little girl, the Writer and the Stalker. In this film, his faith has apparently disappeared and he becomes a fascist. Since no one wants to go with him, he takes people against their will.

Q: *What do you say to people that say* Stalker *is a despairing film?*
T: I don't know. I don't believe it is. I don't believe a work of art can be based on this type of emotion. It has to have a positive, spiritual meaning and contain hope and faith. I don't think my film is despairing, or if it is, it isn't a work of art. Even if it contains moments of despair, it still rises above them. It's a sort of catharsis. It's a tragedy and a tragedy isn't despairing. It's a story of destruction, which leaves the viewer with a sense of hope, because of the catharsis that Aristotle describes. Tragedy purifies man.

Q: *Your film has something of a Platonic dialogue within it, where poetry and philosophy rub shoulders.*
T: Yes, you have this feeling because in fact this isn't a trip but a kind of conversation in which the characters discover who they are. My impression is that true philosophers are always poets and vice versa. I needed images, symbols imbued with emotion, but that doesn't mean that they are devoid of any intellectual content. Any image, however striking, and it ought to be striking, has a very specific and important intellectual content. That's why I can't separate one from the other.

Q: *Why did you make the characters a Writer and a Scientist?*
T: For the Scientist, there was a simple reason. Who is it that could make a bomb? For a scientist, this would be easy technically since he has all the means necessary at his disposal. Given all that, it is not absolutely necessary that he be a scientist. It could have been anyone, but this would have made it difficult to present the story of the bomb.

Q: *And the Writer?*

T: That's a very important character for me. Of course, it could have been someone else. A painter, a musician, a poet, anyone with a spiritual activity. So why not a writer?

Q: *Each of these three characters represent you a little bit. They are each one-third of Tarkovsky, are they not?*

T: Yes, but the one that pleases me the most is the Stalker. He is the best part of me, and also the part that is the least real. I feel very close to the Writer also. He is a character who has lost his way, but I feel he could find a spiritual way out of his predicament. I don't know about the Scientist. He is a very limited person. I wouldn't like to think that I am like him. Yet despite his obvious limitations, he does allow himself to change his mind, and he has an open mind, with the capacity for understanding.

Q: *In this film, as in* The Mirror, *water plays a big role. There are many shots underwater, and with remarkable colors. What do they represent? How did you choose the colors?*

T: I don't know. And I also feel that if we begin to talk about these things, we'll never be able to stop. In any case, when we shot, we approached these issues as painters.

Q: *The ruins, and the rusty objects you filmed underwater—did you find them on location or did you bring them there?*

T: Some were there already, and others we brought.

Q: *How do you see the Zone? As an imaginary place?*

T: I don't know. In a way, it's a product of the Stalker's imagination. We thought about it this way: he was the one who created that place, to bring people and show them around, to convince them of the reality of his creation. Hence, the objects in the water, the fire he lit that was burning unbeknownst to them. I entirely accept the idea that this world was created by the Stalker in order to instill faith—faith in his reality. It was a working hypothesis that we used to create this universe. We even planned to have a variation of the ending in which we would tell the viewer that the Stalker had invented the whole thing, and that he was desperate because people didn't believe in it.

Imagine a very rich man who created, from a little of everything, a world, a house to which he would bring his friends in order to create a certain impression. Obviously, if I were him, I wouldn't say that I've known this place for a long time, that I made it myself. It would be an experience for others, a fascinating sensation. That is the basis of creation in what could be called Stalker's line of work.

Q: *At a certain point there is a line about how intellectuals hope to be paid for the slightest movement of their souls . . .*
T: Yes, that's what the Stalker says at the end. The truth is that in the contemporary world, people want to be paid for everything. Not necessarily literally, with money. But a person who behaves in a moral way wants to be recognized as being a moral person. This is the perspective of modern man, and I believe it results from the loss of a spiritual life.

Q: *Can you tell us about your next film, to be called* A Voyage to Italy?
T: I have just started working on it. I'm afraid to say much because in fact, there isn't much to say. It's too early.

Against Interpretation: An Interview with Andrei Tarkovsky

IAN CHRISTIE/1981

ANDREI TARKOVSKY ARRIVED in London at less than a week's notice to attend the press show of *Stalker* and give a Guardian Lecture at the National Film Theater on 8 February. It was his first visit to Britain and came as a complete surprise to his hosts, the GB-USSR Association, who had been trying to arrange a visit for many years. Despite a reputation for being uncomfortable with publicity and the press, Tarkovsky coped with a full schedule of interviews and eagerly took the opportunity to collect a dossier of Western reviews and cuttings on his work from the BFI Information Library.

His hastily improvised itinerary included trips to see *Mon Oncle d'Amerique* ("not my kind of film, too mechanical") and, more enthusiastically, a cross-section of popular films. He also visited the National Film School and introduced special screenings of *Stalker* at Glasgow and Edinburgh Film Theaters which, like the NFT, were heavily sold out at a few days notice.

The strategy followed in the first part of the NFT interview, before questions from the audience, was to establish some of the basic parameters within which Tarkovsky and all Soviet filmmakers work; partly because so little is known (or finds its way into public knowledge) about the production context in the West, and partly to counter the wholly obfuscatory view of Tarkovsky as "persecuted artist." As evidence

---

From *Framework*, no.14 (1981). Reprinted by permission.

to the contrary, he confirmed in conversation that he had been able to re-shoot a substantial part of *Stalker* when dissatisfied with a first version. Tatiana Storchak of Goskino, who accompanied him, explained that he has often taken part in public discussions of his work in the Soviet Union. The point of course is not to deny that he has been heavily criticized for obscurity and elitism—witness the discussion in *Iskusstkvo Kino* in 1975 cited by Herbert Marshall in his *Sight and Sound* article, Spring 1976—but clearly Tarkovsky is also a respected and approved filmmaker who has at least the same opportunity to work as his Western contemporaries—indeed rather greater, looking at the state of European art cinema. His value in earning cultural prestige and hard currency can also hardly be denied.

Inevitably a public interview conducted spontaneously through an interpreter produces a rather unsatisfactory text for reproduction and, stripped of the passion and humor of Tarkovsky's performance, parts of it may appear simplistic. But against this must be set the serious lack of material in English on any of the Soviet filmmakers of Tarkovsky's generation. Without such encounters, there can be no basis for understanding the sheer difference and otherness of Soviet cinema; and Tarkovsky's position, however idiosyncratic, can only appear highly provocative in the context of official Soviet aesthetics.

IAN CHRISTIE: *Does the response to your films outside the USSR mean a lot to you?*
T: Of course I am very pleased that people see my films and like them in the West. But it is much more important what people think of my films in the Soviet Union, because I work in my own country and the opinion of my own people is very important to me.

Q: *What is the normal process of setting up a film in the Soviet industry?*
T: I work at the Mosfilm Studio which does not employ writers so we commission screenplays. The studio buys screenplays in which Mosfilm directors have some interest. Sometimes screenplays are also prepared by the directors themselves, or writers prepare them at the request of directors. Mosfilm is divided into several so-called "creative units" where the quality of screenplays is discussed: the profitability of each project is considered and then production is started. When Goskino,

the state cinema organization (Ministry of Cinema) approves the production of a particular screenplay, the state bank automatically advances funds and then we start preliminary work on the film, like anywhere else.

Mosfilm is subordinate to Goskino, but it has all the facilities needed for production—workshops, studios, laboratory—so that nothing has to be done outside. And when we are actually filming there aren't the same time restrictions as elsewhere. The finished film is submitted to the organizations which approve its production. First its quality is discussed within the particular unit at Mosfilm by a "creative council," which consists of the writers, director and the whole creative crew of the film. By this time it is too late anyway to make changes in the film, and it is submitted to Goskino, where it is viewed and assigned to a particular category. Depending on the category chosen, members of the crew are paid for their work and the number of copies to be made is decided.

Q: *What problems can arise at this stage?*
T: The only thing that can prevent a film being shown is misunderstanding, unless it turns out to be a total failure that nothing can save. Sometimes a film is perceived in a way that its maker didn't foresee. A polemic can arise which then conflicts with the logic of the film's release but this is very rare. As regards my own problems, these were mainly with *Andrei Roublev*. To this day I cannot understand why there was such a delay in releasing the film. Maybe sometime in the future a historian of Soviet cinema will discover the true reason. I think many of the problems in this case were due to the fear of those involved with the film's release.

Q: *Is it possible to make a low-budget film, not intended for wide release?*
T: For us there is no real connection between the size of the budget and release, and there have been cases where huge sums of money were spent on films which hardly anyone saw, and equally, films costing a few kopecks have proved extremely popular. There isn't the same connection between production and distribution that you have: since everything is in the hands of the state, losses on expensive films can be balanced against gains on cheap films. So you see there are great possibilities when all the films belong to one organization.

Q: *Both* Andrei Roublev *and* Solaris *can be seen as variations on familiar Soviet genres: the historical fresco and the science-fiction drama. Was it your intention to work against the normal expectations involved in these genres?*

T: I do not believe that the cinema has genres—the cinema is *itself* a genre. Once we start talking about genre, we are dealing with a systematization arising from the cinema as a commercial enterprise. But cinema is a high art, a deeply poetic art: it doesn't need any schemas to violate its potential. The dilemma of the filmmaker boils down to the fact that he's deeply dependent on money. Cinema is the only art that has its origins in the bazaar. However, a few masterpieces have emerged during its short history which prove that it is capable of higher things. When I made *Andrei Roublev*, I never thought of it as a historical film, nor of *Solaris* as a science-fiction film—although I do feel that *Solaris* is the least successful of my films because I was never able to eliminate the science-fiction association. Stanislaw Lem (the author of the novel) saw the script and was worried. He threatened to withdraw his permission for the film, so we prepared another script which I hoped we would be able to quietly drop during shooting. But we didn't succeed.

Q: *You followed many interests before entering the cinema: you attended music school, studied painting and Arabic, and went prospecting in Siberia, all before you enrolled at VGIK, the cinema school. What made you want to become a director?*

T: You can't decide to be a director, you've got to become one. If I taught in a film school I would dissuade students from trying to become directors. No one knows the labor and struggle that is involved: the real work of the director is not with the cast on the set: it is no different from the inner creative work carried out by the poet and the composer, but this is far from the popular view.

Q: *What did you gain from your studies with Mikhail Romm at VGIK over the six years of the course?*

T: One of the French kings—was it Dominic XV perhaps?—claimed that he did everything by not hindering anything. Mikhail Romm was a teacher who did everything possible to preserve the individual in each of us. He was a unique teacher in that sense: he didn't try to teach us our profession, since we would learn it anyway once we started to work.

I could teach anyone the profession of film director in three months, but it wouldn't make him an artist. Mikhail Romm taught us to respect ourselves and I regard him as one of our most outstanding teachers.

(Tarkovsky talked about his methods of working with collaborators, building up intuitive relationships, before the last reel of Mirror *was shown).*

Q: *You have described* Mirror *as a story told by a man who becomes seriously ill. How do you think this affects audiences' understanding of the film?*

T: People ask themselves serious questions at different times, and especially in the face of death. The logic of our hero's reminiscences is on the moment at which it all happens, and on the reason behind these memories. That is why we had to show our hero at a time of serious illness—if he had been healthy and full of joy, then he would have remembered different things and in a different way. But I want to emphasize that the film was not constructed in this way for dry, dramatic reasons. It is important to see our hero in an extreme psychological situation, so that we don't feel his illness is entirely accidental. And it is the kind of illness where we don't know if he will survive, although this is not important to the meaning of the film—if there is any meaning!

(In response to a question from the audience on the allegorical interpretation of his films and on a rumored Dostoevsky adaptation)

T: My objective is to create my own world and these images which we create mean nothing more than the images which they are. We have forgotten how to relate emotionally to art: we treat it like editors, searching in it for that which the artist has supposedly hidden. It is actually much simpler than that, otherwise art would have no meaning. You have to be a child—incidentally children understand my pictures very well, and I haven't met a single serious critic who could stand knee-high to those children. We think that art demands special knowledge; we demand some higher meaning from an author, but the work must act directly on our hearts or it has no meaning at all.

I wouldn't like to describe my pictures as allegorical: they talk about things that disturb me. If my account is allegorical, that is not my intention—there is no ulterior motive to reveal a hidden meaning. In

Moscow I often meet viewers and I usually fight with them and try to make them like children, generally without success.

I am writing a screenplay based on *The Idiot* and it's very hard work. Many things have been ascribed to Dostoevsky which just aren't true. For example, people everywhere—including Moscow—think of him as a religious writer. But it does not seem to have occurred to them that he was not so much religious as one of the first to express the drama of the man in whom the organ of belief has atrophied. He dealt with the tragedy of the loss of spirituality. All his heroes are people who would *like* to believe but cannot, and it seems to me that it is this concern with spiritual emptiness, with the crisis of religiosity, that explains the enormous interest in Dostoevsky here in the West. He managed never to talk about this directly, but all his life he suffered because he was unable to believe. He always behaved like a believer, but he was unable to confess to anyone: he would have regarded it as improper to do so. This is the point of view I want to take in treating Prince Myshkin.

(In response to a question about the primacy of emotional response to his films)

T: What matters to me is that the feeling excited by my films should be universal. An artistic image is capable of arousing identical feelings in viewers, while the thoughts that come later may be very different. If you start to search for a meaning during the film you will miss everything that happens. The ideal viewer is someone who watches a film like a traveler watching the country he is passing through: because the effect of an artistic image is an extra-mental type of communication. There are some artists who attach symbolic meaning to their images, but that is not possible for me. Zen poets have a good way of dealing with this: they work to eliminate any possibility of interpretation, and in the process a parallel arises between the real world and what the artist creates in his work.

What then is the purpose of this activity? It seems to me that the purpose of art is to prepare the human soul for the perception of good. The soul opens up under the influence of an artistic image, and it is for this reason that we say it helps us to communicate—but it is communication in the highest sense of the word. I could not imagine a work of art that would prompt a person to do something bad. There can be no talk of art in relation to films like *The Exterminator*. My purpose as far as possible is to make films that will help people to live, even if they sometimes cause unhappiness—and I don't mean the sort of tears that *Kramer vs. Kramer* produces. Perhaps you have noticed that the more pointless people's tears during a film, the more profound the reason for these tears. I am not talking about sentimentality, but about how art can reach to the depths of the human soul and leave man defenseless against good.

(A question implying that his images were more valuable than his words provoked laughter when Tarkovsky feigned alarm—"You mean in my films?")

T: The point is that speech and words are merely a part of the world around us and why should we reject that part of the world? That would be pure formalism.

(Did he regret that other filmmakers do not combine color and black and white within their films?)

T: I don't know any directors who choose to make black and white films today. Viewers like colored pictures, but strangely enough I believe that color can be much less realistic than black and white, because in life we don't normally think about color. Whereas in the cinema the viewer immediately notices that the image is in color, and to what extent, and this conceals the conventional nature of color film. For me, black and white has an unforgettable and highly expressive quality, and I will continue to make films that include a lot of black and white. I think that the cinema may even return to black and white, if it survives at all.

(Which Soviet filmmakers does he admire most?)

T: I regard the Georgian Iosseliani and Sergei Paradjanov as the best Soviet filmmakers, and I would place third the Leningrad director Guerman, who made *Twenty Days Without War*.

Tarkovsky's Translations

PHILIP STRICK/1981

THANKS TO THE TUGGING of some obscure strings, Andrei Tarkovsky popped up in London just as *Stalker* began its run at the Academy earlier this year. He was known, of course, to have visited Italy and France during the past decade, but he had begun to seem one of those Russians the West would seldom be allowed to meet, a status that does wonders for the reputation. Now here he was, abruptly in our midst for his first London visit, and the word got around fast. In a handful of days they fed him a conveyor belt of journalists and disciples, and at brief notice the NFT was wall-to-wall packed for his appearance.

Joining the queue as one who had theorized at some length about him while distributing *Solaris*, I was able in conspiracy with Charles and Kitty Cooper of Contemporary Films to sneak him off for a meal. Small and bristling, casual in no-nonsense blue denims, he moved in jerks as if some impatient editor kept clipping out frames from his personal time sequence. With considerable eloquence on his own part and that of the two official interpreters, he demonstrated an inclination to say as little as possible about anything specific; and while it was evident that he recognized some English here and there, any direct conversation was out.

A few points of fact nevertheless brought down some myths. No, *Solaris* was not cut for release outside Russia; what you see, lacunae and all, is at two hours and forty-eight minutes precisely what he intended. No, he had nothing whatever to do with *First Teacher*, which he is usually credited as having written with Mikhalkov-Konchalovsky alongside

From *Sight and Sound* 50, no. 3 (Summer 1981): 152–53. Reprinted by permission.

their collaboration on *Roublev*. No, *The Mirror* was in no way suppressed by the authorities—on the contrary, they opened the Moscow cinema earlier in the day during its first run (7:00 A.M., at which hour it must have been something of a mixed blessing), to meet the public demand for extra screenings.

Another surprise was the revelation that because of a laboratory pro-cessing error, much of *Stalker* had been shot twice. "Frustrating, yes, but it's a much better film as a result. Things changed the second time around—a woman can never give birth to the same child twice—but I'm more satisfied with the final product than I am with any of my other films." Did the processing error account for the intermingling of color and monochrome? "No, that was all intentional. I love black and white cinema; I feel as if I discovered it. Audiences are supposed to prefer color films, but I believe that color is much less realistic than black and white. We don't normally notice color, except in the cinema where it's some-how exaggerated. So the most 'real' images on film are in monochrome." Did this mean that the Zone in *Stalker*, which is (mostly) in color by con-trast with the drab world outside, is intended to be unreal? "The Zone is a diseased area, abandoned; certainly there's an unreality about it. The use of color could well mean it's unreal, but I don't know for sure."

Which brought us bang up against the much-argued problem of what, in Tarkovsky's films, one *can* know for sure. On this subject, he switched into overdrive (his NFT audience got the same treatment) while both interpreters at once struggled to keep up with the pace. "Everybody asks me what things mean in my films. This is terrible! An artist doesn't have to answer for his meanings. I don't think so deeply about my work—I don't *know* what my symbols may represent. What matters to me is that they arouse feelings, any feelings you like, based on whatever your inner response might be. If you *look* for a meaning, you'll miss everything that happens. Thinking during a film interferes with your experience of it. Take a watch to pieces, it doesn't work. Similarly with a work of art, there's no way it can be analyzed without destroying it."

Wouldn't he concede that in the autobiographical aspects of *The Mirror* there may be incidents and images which meant more to Tarkovsky than to anyone else? He admitted, with regret, that the film had lost him a lot of friends. "It was rather silly; they reproached me for

being too personal in telling my own story. But, if I show things that I
didn't understand when they happened, how can I explain them now?
People are intent on finding something in my work that I've 'con-
cealed,' but it would be strange to make a film and hide one's thoughts.
My images mean nothing more than they are." But surely, I persisted,
he had a purpose in mind when arranging, for example, that a bird
should land on a boy's head in *The Mirror*? And after some exasperation
and sighing from the interpreters, purpose there proved to have been.
"My wife," he said, "attracts birds. When we walk in the forest, birds fly
close to her—she is like them, a part of nature. Some country people
even call her a sorceress. Now, I know there is no malice in her at all,
birds will never approach an evil being. In the film, the child has just
misbehaved, so to show the audience he isn't some kind of delinquent,
beyond hope, I illustrate with the bird a hint of his true nature."

As an explanation, it was not without impact. And with break-
through achieved, Tarkovsky began to produce meanings quite readily.
Some were more plausible than others. The final sequence of *Solaris*?
"Kris, the astronaut, has been recreated by the Ocean—the materialization of his homesickness has been taken from him and reconstructed
on the planet." The wife/mother in *The Mirror* floating in midair above
the bed? "Neither nightmare nor symbol; a sense of floating is what we
all feel when all our support has gone." (And no, he was not going to
tell me how he achieved the shot, other than that it was extremely simple to do.) The seemingly telekinetic ability of the child in *Stalker*? "We
don't know ourselves all that well; sometimes we manifest forces that
can't be measured by normal standards. I expect something like that,"
he added thoughtfully, "to happen at any time."

Perhaps, after all, Tarkovsky's images were best left ambiguous. At
the NFT, refusing to be interrupted in mid-flow for the obligatory film
extracts, he had the last word: "We've forgotten to relate emotionally
to art—we treat it like editors, when everything's really very simple.
Children have that simplicity and they understand my films very well. I
haven't met a single serious critic who stands knee-high to those children when it comes to accepting my films for what they are."

Tarkovsky in Italy

TONY MITCHELL/1982

"I AM STARTING WORK on my new film at the end of September [1982], and I don't quite know how to cope with it," Andrei Tarkovsky said. "It is being produced by RAI and Gaumont, in collaboration with Sovin Film in Moscow, and it has taken three and a half years to reach the point where I am now. I already feel as if I have shot the film I don't know how many times. It's difficult to remain fresh. In Moscow I never had to think about money because I didn't have to go out looking for it; but now I know how it feels to be in that situation, and it's very difficult to remain yourself. My films have always been the films I wanted to make. I haven't experienced my Italian colleagues' terrible difficulties. In fact, though, I am working under very good conditions. My screenplay has already been drafted, so that's a thing of the past, which means I'm inclined to modify it during shooting, as I did in my last film, *Stalker*. The problem is that I have never had enough time for the editing. I hope I will this time, since it doesn't really cost anything."

Andrei Tarkovsky's *Nostalgia*, scripted by Tonino Guerra, regular collaborator with Antonioni and more recently with Rosi, is finally under way. Using an Italian crew and the actors Oleg Yankovsky, who was in *The Mirror*, Erland Josephson, and Domiziana Giordano, the film is the first by a Russian director to be made for European television. It will cost some £500,000 and will be shot in color on location in Tuscany, Florence, Pisa, Rome, Milan, Venice, Ravenna, and Moscow. A spring release is planned with television screenings in 1984.

From *Sight and Sound* 52, no. 1 (Winter 1982/1983). Reprinted by permission.

Tarkovsky describes *Nostalgia* as "a simple love story." Andrei Gorgiakhov (Yankovsky), a Russian university teacher, comes to Italy for the first time to see the architecture on which he has for years been lecturing. He develops an unrequited affection for his interpreter and guide (Domiziana Giordano); and he discovers a type of alter ego in Domenico (Josephson), a Tuscan professor of mathematics, who is regarded as a madman because he believes the world is coming to an end.

At an RAI press conference in Rome to announce the start of production, Tarkovsky had this to say: "*Nostalgia* is about the impossibility of people living together without really knowing one another, and about the problems arising from the necessity of getting to know one another. It's very simple to make acquaintances, much more difficult to arrive at a deeper knowledge of another person. Then there is an aspect of the film which is less evident on the surface, concerning the impossibility of importing or exporting culture, of appropriating another people's culture. We Russians can claim to know Dante and Petrarch, just as you Italians can claim to know Pushkin, but this is really impossible—you have to be of the same nationality. The reproduction and distribution of culture is harmful to its essence and spreads only a superficial impression. It is not possible to teach one person the culture of another.

"In the film, the interpreter Eugenia asks, 'What do you have to do to understand another people?' And Andrei replies, 'Destroy the borders.' It's a complex global problem which is either resolved on a simple level or not at all. On a simple level it can be resolved by a child, but on a more complex level it involves self-understanding. Andrei tries to unload these problems on his alter ego the madman. Andrei is searching for the truth and at times feels it is useless to teach something he doesn't know at first hand. In the madman he finds someone who is convinced about his actions, who claims to know how to save the world and acts accordingly. Domenico is like a defenceless child who acts without reflection, and so in a way represents what is missing in Andrei."

The character of Domenico was inspired by a newspaper story which Guerra came across after he had already partially drafted the screenplay. It was, Tarkovsky said, a lucky find which synthesized an important aspect of the film. "Guerra is a poet of rare talent, capable of making great discoveries. Luckily I work in the cinema, whereas he's a poet, so I don't have to envy him." Tarkovsky had originally planned to shoot a considerable portion of the film in Moscow, but agreements with Sovin Film broke down and he had to halve the footage earmarked for the Moscow scenes. "Destiny gave us a hand. The house we found in Tuscany is much more interesting cinematically than the Moscow locations, and I'm very glad to be able to expand this little corner of Russia in Italy."

Does water still obsess Tarkovsky? "Water is a mysterious element, a single molecule of which is very photogenic," Tarkovsky said. "It can convey movement and a sense of change and flux. There will be a lot of it in *Nostalgia*. Maybe it has subconscious echoes—perhaps my love of water arises from some atavistic memory or some ancestral transmigration."

Questioned about a possible conflict between the "pessimism" of his films and the "optimism" of the Italian way of life, and about the difficulty Italians find in understanding his films, Tarkovsky said, "I am not without optimism. My film is, after all, a love story which is relatively simple and comprehensible. But at the same time I've tried to get to the bottom of the more profound and disturbing aspects beneath its surface. Pessimism arises from worry and the complexity of the problems one poses oneself. These problems can't simply be resolved by a joyous attitude to the world. I'm interested in characters who are worried about the state of the world, and perhaps this sometimes involves too much complexity.

"Cinema is an art form which involves a high degree of tension, which may not generally be comprehensible. It's not that I don't want to be understood, but I can't, like Spielberg, say, make a film for the general public—I'd be mortified if I discovered I could. If you want to reach a general audience, you have to make films like *Star Wars* and *Superman*, which have nothing to do with art. This doesn't mean I treat the public like idiots, but I certainly don't take pains to please them. I don't know why I'm always so defensive in front of journalists—I might need you one of these days, especially if my film gets the same kind of distribution as Angelopoulos!"

Tarkovsky expanded his ideas at the conference "Cinema Thieves—International Intrigue" held at the Centro Palatino in Rome on 9 September 1982. He presented clips from *Seven Samurai, Mouchette, Nazarin,* and *La Notte,* the films which had made the most incisive impression on him, as opposed to having influenced him.

ANDREI TARKOVSKY: "The problem of influence, influx, or reciprocal activity is complex. Cinema doesn't exist in a vacuum—one has colleagues and so influences are inevitable. So what is influence or influx? The artist's choice of the environment in which he works, the people with whom he works, is like his choice of a dish at a restaurant. As for the influence of Kurosawa, Mizoguchi, Bresson, Buñuel, Bergman, and Antonioni on my work, it is not influence in the sense of 'imitation'— from my point of view this would be impossible since imitation has nothing to do with the aims of cinema. One has to find one's own language through which to express oneself. To me influx means being in the company of people whom I admire and esteem.

"If I notice that a frame or a sequence echoes another director, I try to avoid it and modify the scene. This happens only very rarely, as for example in *The Mirror* when I set up a frame in which the leading woman was in a room and her mother [sic] in the next. There was a close-up of the two women, although it was a panoramic shot, and the mother was looking in the mirror. In fact the whole scene was shot through a mirror, although the mirror did not actually exist, and the woman was looking directly into the room. There was only the impression of a mirror. I realized that this type of scene could have come straight out of Bergman. Nonetheless, I decided to shoot the scene as it was, as an acknowledgment of, or nod towards, my colleague.

"Without the directors I've mentioned, and with the addition of Dovzhenko, there wouldn't be any cinema. Everyone naturally looks for his own original style, but without these directors providing a context or background, cinema wouldn't be the same. Many filmmakers seem to be going through a very difficult period at the moment. In Italy, cinema is in a predicament. My Italian colleagues, and I'm talking about some of the best-known names in the cinema, tell me that Italian cinema has ceased to exist. Cinema audiences are, of course, a major factor in this. For a long time cinema followed public taste, but now the public doesn't want to see a certain type of film, which is all to the good really.

"There are two basic categories of film directors. One consists of those who seek to imitate the world in which they live, the other are those who seek to create their own world. The second category contains the poets of the cinema, Bresson, Dovzhenko, Mizoguchi, Bergman, Buñuel, and Kurosawa, the cinema's most important names. The work of these filmmakers is difficult to distribute: it reflects their inner aspirations, and this always runs counter to public taste. This does not mean that the filmmakers don't want to be understood by their audience. But rather that they themselves try to pick up on and understand the inner feelings of the audience.

"Despite the current plight of the cinema, film remains an art form, and every art form is specific, with a content which doesn't correspond to the essence of other forms. For example, photography can be an art form, as the genius of Cartier-Bresson shows, but it is not comparable to painting because it's not in competition with painting. The question that filmmakers must ask themselves is, what distinguishes cinema from the other arts? To me cinema is unique in its dimension of time. This doesn't mean it develops in time—so do music, theater, and ballet. I mean time in the literal sense. What is a frame, the interval between 'Action' and 'Cut'? Film fixes reality in a sense of time—it's a way of conserving time. No other art form can fix and stop time like this. Film is a mosaic made up of time. This involves gathering elements. Imagine three or four directors or cameramen shooting the same material for an hour, each with his own particular vision. The result would be three or four totally different types of film—each person would throw out some bits and keep others and make his own film. Despite the fixing of time involved in film, the director can always elaborate his material and express his own creativity through it.

"The cinema is going through a bad period in terms of aesthetics. Filming in color is regarded as getting as close as possible to reality. But I look on color as a blind alley. Every art form tries to arrive at truth and seeks to form a generalization. Using color is related to how one perceives the real world. Filming a scene in color involves organizing and structuring a frame, realizing that all the world enclosed in this frame is in color and making the audience aware of this. The advantage of black and white is that it is extremely expressive and it doesn't distract the audience's attention.

"You can find examples of expressive modes in color cinema, but most directors who are aware of this problem have always tried to film in black and white. No one has succeeded in creating a different perspective in color film or in making it as effective as black and white. Italian neorealism is not only important for the fact that it turned a new page in the cinema by exploring the problems of everyday life, but also, essentially, because it did this in black and white. Truth in life doesn't necessarily correspond to truth in art, and now color film has become a purely commercial phenomenon. The cinema went through a period of trying to create a new vision through color, but this hasn't amounted to anything. The cinema has become too glossy, which means the film I am watching becomes quite different for a person sitting in the other corner.

"The film clips which I am showing represent what is closest to my heart. They are examples of a form of thought and how this thought is expressed through film. In Bresson's *Mouchette* the way in which the girl commits suicide is particularly striking. In *Seven Samurai*, in the sequence in which the youngest member of the group is afraid, we see how Kurosawa transmits this sense of fear. The boy is trembling in the grass, but we don't see him trembling, we see the grass and flowers trembling. We see a battle in the rain and when the character played by Toshiro Mifune dies we see him fall and his legs become covered with mud. He dies before our eyes.

"In Buñuel's *Nazarin*, we see the injured prostitute being helped by Nazarin and how she drinks the water from the bowl. The final sequence of Antonioni's *La Notte* is perhaps the only episode in the whole history of cinema in which a love scene became a necessity and took on the semblance of a spiritual act. It's a unique sequence in which physical closeness has great significance. The characters have exhausted their feelings for each other but are still very close to each other. As a friend of mine said once, more than five years with my husband is like incest. These characters have no exit from their closeness. We see them desperately trying to save each other, as if they were dying.

"When I start shooting, I always look at the films I like, by the directors I consider to be in 'my group'—not to imitate them, but to savor their atmosphere. It's no accident that all the clips I'm showing are in black and white. They are important because the directors transform something close to them into something precious. And all these scenes are unique in that they are not like events in everyday life. This is the stamp of the great artist, showing us our interior world. All these scenes cater to the audience's desire by conserving beauty rather than giving enjoyment. These days it's extremely difficult to deal with this type of subject, it's almost absurd even to talk about it—no one would give you a sou. But the cinema will only continue to exist thanks to these poets.

"To make a film you need money. To write a poem all you need is pen and paper. This puts cinema at a disadvantage. But I think cinema is invincible, and I bow down to all the directors who try to realize their own films despite everything. All the films from which I've shown examples have their own rhythm. (Nowadays, it seems, most directors use rapid, short scenes, and directors who use cutting and speed are considered to be really professional.) The aim of any true director is to express truth, but what do producers care? In the 1940s, there was a survey in America ranking professions according to stress. This was at the time of Hiroshima and pilots came out on top. The second place went to film directors. It's almost a suicidal profession.

"I've just come back from Venice, where I was on the festival jury, and I can testify to the complete decadence of current cinema. Venice was a piteous spectacle. To understand and accept a film like Fassbinder's *Querelle* requires, I believe, a totally different type of spirituality. Marcel Carné obviously accepted it more than I did. I think it's a manifestation of an anti-artistic phenomenon; its concerns are sociological and sexual problems. It would have been profoundly unjust to have given the film an award simply because it was Fassbinder's last film—I think he has made much better films than this. The present crisis in cinema isn't important, however, because the arts always go through periods of crisis and then there is a revival. Just because you can't make a film doesn't mean the cinema is dead.

"At its best, cinema comes between music and poetry. It has reached as high a level as any art form. And as an art form it has consolidated itself. Antonioni's *L'Avventura* was made a long time ago, but it gives the impression of having been made today. It's a miraculous film and has not aged a bit. Perhaps it is not the sort of film one would make today but it still has that freshness. My Italian colleagues are going through a very bad period. Neorealism and the great directors seem to have disappeared. Producers are like drug-pushers, they only want to make money, but most of them don't last long. I almost disowned the version of *Solaris* which was shown in Italy. But now the company which distributed it no longer exists, which seems to be the fate of most distributors."

Nostalgia's Black Tone

HERVÉ GUIBERT/1983

Q: *In Paris I was told that Andrei Tarkovsky prefers to have a French-Italian interpreter rather than a French-Russian one, that he suspects all Russian interpreters to be working for the KGB.*

That must be a joke, says Andrei Tarkovsky, according to the interpreter who adds, "Me, I'm a Polish refugee since 1969, Italian citizen."

Q: *So, what is the story of* Nostalghia?
T: Only a few days separate us from its projection at Cannes. I have practically nothing to say about the film, and I don't wish to anticipate. I am however able to give some concrete information which will be able to prepare the spectator but which will not convey to him the film as such. Its director himself hasn't yet seen it finished.

Q: *Just the same, you know what it is you wanted to express?*
T: Simply put, I wanted to speak about that which is called "nostalgia," but I mean the word in its Russian sense, that is to say, a fatal disease. I wanted to show psychological traits typically Russian, in the tradition of Dostoevsky. The Russian term is difficult to translate: it could be compassion, but it's even stronger than that. It's identifying oneself with the suffering of another man, in a passionate way.

From *Le Monde*, 12 May 1983, 13. Reprinted by permission. Translated from French by John Gianvito.

Q: *The suffering of which man?*
T: In principal, it's a question of any man, of the relationship between men in general, but naturally this feeling of compassion becomes extremely strong when it's a question of a man you are close to.

Q: *But who suffers and of what?*
T: I have three characters: a traveling Russian poet, his translator, and an Italian who they meet in the Italian provinces. The film tells of the compassion of a Russian towards an Italian.

Q: *The Italian suffers more than the Russian?*
T: I think so, yes. But I can't go into the details without touching upon the subject of the film which should be left up to the viewers. Besides, the subject has no decisive importance, because the film doesn't base its argument directly on it, it's formed from other material. This is the first time, in my experience, that I have felt to such a degree that the film itself was capable of being the expression of psychological states of the author. The central character assumes the role of the alter-ego of the director.

Q: *How were you able to distance yourself from the subject and yet draw nearer to yourself?*
T: This wasn't premeditated. It happened during the shooting, I wasn't consciously willing it. I discovered it in the material.

Q: *Is it the actors who provided this identification?*
T: One can't underestimate the importance of actors, but I don't think that they are responsible for it. It's like a coincidence: that which I wanted to show suddenly approximated states of the soul that I had lived during my stay in Italy. It would be difficult to separate out the factors for this situation.

Q: *Every man is aware of his suffering; with you, where does it originate?*
T: In the fact that man is consumed by material things. Throughout the course of history, progress has advanced by gigantic strides in comparison to spiritual development. Man hasn't taken into account that this growth is out of harmony with his spirit.

Q: *In what sense do you speak of man in general?*

T: In general, man has the tendency to speak about others rather than of himself, to consider others more than himself, in both good and negative ways. Man is rather indifferent with regard to his own fate. Egoism doesn't mean self-love, it's something completely opposite. Everything depends upon where man finds meaning in his life. If we think that man doesn't belong to himself, egoism can't be the expression of self-love. One begins to think of oneself fairly late: sooner or later in life, one has to become self-aware.

Q: *What is it that prevents this?*

T: Just this necessity of living in a material way in this material world. Not everyone succeeds in grasping that they also have a spiritual life.

Q: *How, in your own life, was this asserted or confirmed?*

T: I don't recall when I was consciously aware of this spiritual being, but I possessed some buds of awareness, and I had the impression that they would develop by themselves. Sometimes I felt someone taking me by the hand and guiding me.

Q: *Is this a good thing or not?*

T: It's a sensation that has nothing to do with pleasure or fear. Rather it's a feeling of security, assurance, nearing a state of happiness that was unknown to me until then. One no longer feels oneself a person abandoned and alone.

Q: *Do you deeply feel yourself an exile, with all its mythology?*

T: I'm unable to speak objectively about finding myself in exile. I came to Rome in March of last year in order to direct a film. I had a contract in collaboration with RAI (Italian television); I am an immigrant worker.

Q: *Within the Soviet Union do you have the feeling of being a privileged individual?*

T: No, fortunately not.

Q: *How are your films received there?*

T: The official viewpoint is that they are difficult to understand. Sergei Bondarchuk expressed this idea in Italy during a press conference.

Nevertheless, young people especially view my films with enormous interest. I would even say that there's a contradiction between that which Bondarchuk declares and the truth.

Q: *Who is Bondarchuk?*
T: He is the greatest Soviet director. He's been awarded every possible prize and official honor in the USSR. It's too bad you don't know him.

Q: *Are you never afraid?*
T: The same as anyone. From time to time I feel fear.

Q: *Is life in Rome more comfortable for you?*
T: In general, I try to flee from the vanities of society life, so intense in capital cities. From this viewpoint, I'm obligated to have to see more people in Rome, to maintain more contacts than in my own country.

Q: *Why have you chosen Italy?*
T: I had been here several times beforehand: I was understanding the milieu better. It seemed natural for me to return here. Apart from Russia, it's the country where I feel the best. I have difficulty explaining it: I believe it's connected to the particular nature of Italian life; even its chaos has personality, vitality. There isn't this "metaphysical" quality of the Nordic countries. And the Eastern indifference toward materialism is the attitude closest to me. In a spiritual sense, the East, through its tradition and its culture, is much nearer the truth than the West.

Q: *Being exiled in Italy draws on a whole literary tradition in Russia . . .*
T: The general ambience produced by Italy, its surface, seems to intensify creativity. The spiritual realm finds itself stimulated by the cultural tradition, which one perceives in a physical way, like a weight. Perhaps I'm mistaken, but this pressure seems connected to this other sensation of not being all that at ease. One feels that one's under the influence of the residue of powerful emotions that existed in the center of the Mediterranean. They trouble the spirit. A lot of my Italian friends find it difficult to live in Rome and do everything they possibly can to try to live closer to nature. For me, it's not the life of the big city like Paris or Moscow which creates the pressure. It's something else: Rome isn't a

city in the way Milan is, it bears the responsibility of heredity, it supports all the layers of centuries past. Elsewhere we live in the precise moment where we're living. For example, when I went to London, I felt as if in the country or in the desert. I don't want to say that the absence or presence of the past is either beneficial or inauspicious.

Q: *When the writer Isaac Babel discovered the bay of Naples, in front of the first palm tree, he exclaimed, "This is Paradise!" But outside of his country, the writing came to a sudden halt. His Parisian stories, for instance, are inferior. And he says it in his correspondence: "I need snow and proletarians in order to write." He's not only a political hostage, but a hostage of his birthplace.*

T: I understand this very well. Despite the fact that Gogol had written *Dead Souls* in Rome, he found it difficult to work there. He liked Italy enormously and several times had requested permission of the Russian authorities to settle there, arguing the fragility of his health and the harshness of the climate. Pushkin also would have worked abroad, but the Czar never allowed him. On the other hand, if one thinks about Bunin, who was acquainted with the situation of exile and who suffered from it, it was in Paris and in Grasse that he produced his most beautiful stories. One falls back upon the material problems in our life. We tend to think that the relationships between members of the same family are the most essential, but they are also the ones which provoke the greatest suffering. Who said that we should live life only in the pursuit of pleasure? I find this assertion ridiculous and wrong.

Q: *But your geographic displacement, has it led to a deviation of your working methods: the language, voices, even the color of the air or surface textures are different . . .*

T: I have the reputation of being a pessimist. When I was able to see the film I directed here, I was myself touched by its sadness, by its dark tone. This isn't exactly pessimism since the film isn't constructed upon material relations. But one couldn't say that I took on the traits of joy and gaiety of Italy. Perhaps this is the fault of impatience and intolerance. It's true that joyful people provoke a certain irritation in me, I can't bear to be around them. Only truly perfect souls ought to have the right to be joyful, or children, or the elderly. But joyful people, generally, lack their qualities. I think joy is lack of understanding of the situation in which we find ourselves.

Q: *Yilmaz Guney, the author of* Yol, *is also an exiled filmmaker. This year he presents at Cannes,* The Wall, *a Turkish film directed in the French provinces . . .*
T: This is a false situation. I don't believe that material differences between living conditions in countries has any excessive influence on human nature. Now, more than in times past, we don't attach importance to the development of the soul. On the contrary, it would seem that we're trying hard to debase the soul. We sink into materiality like flies in honey. And we feel comfortable there. Is progress leading us in the right direction? If one compares the number of victims caused by the Inquisition to those victims of concentration camps, one would say that the Inquisition was a Golden Age. The greatest absurdity of our times is thinking that, united together, people of a spiritually inferior character are able to bring happiness to the rest of humanity. Again, men thinking to save others. But in order to save others, it's necessary to first save oneself. It's necessary to possess spiritual strength. Without it, that which aims to help transforms into imposition, into violence. If every man was able to save himself, there wouldn't be any need to save others. We love to give advice, to instruct, while, as far as we ourselves are concerned, we overlook the gravest sins.

Q: *Isn't the concept of evil more of a political notion than a material one?*
T: Politics is a material activity of man.

Q: *You would prefer to defend spirituality as opposed to emotion?*
T: Emotion is the enemy of spirituality. Herman Hesse said a good thing about this with regard to passion. In *The Glass-Bead Game*, he wrote that passion is a friction between the outer world and the inner world, the soul. It seems to me that Hesse properly considered emotions as the encounter of man with material reality. Emotionality has nothing to do with true spirituality.

Q: *Would your films prove that you're attracted to metaphor?*
T: Our life is a metaphor, from the beginning until the end. Everything that surrounds us is a metaphor.

Q: *But in your films, what part of the real, what part of the unreal, and what part of yourself do you place there?*
T: It's impossible to create something unreal. Everything is real and unfortunately we aren't able to abandon reality. We can express ourselves toward the world that exists in a poetic way or a purely descriptive manner. Personally, I prefer to express myself in a metaphoric way. I insist on saying metaphoric and not symbolic. The symbol intrinsically comprises a specific meaning, an intellectual formula, while the metaphor is the image itself. It's an image that possesses the same characteristics as the world it represents. Contrary to the symbol, its meaning is undefined. We aren't able to speak about a world that is truly boundless utilizing means which themselves are definite and restricted. We can analyze a formula, that is to say, a symbol, but a metaphor is an entity unto itself, a monomial. If one tries to describe it, immediately it falls to pieces.

Q: *Haven't you attempted to recreate around you, through familiar objects, your Russian world, and, on the larger scale, through film?*
T: Perhaps that's what's been produced, some people have mentioned it, but it's unconsciously that I surrounded myself with things that reminded me of my country. This isn't really a good thing. Man ought to be able to live without anything. Tolstoy said that in order to be happy one mustn't wish for impossible things. It's very simple. The problem is knowing how to differentiate possible and impossible things.

Q: *But what of this photo of a dog there above you?*
T: It's a Russian dog, a member of my family who has remained in Russia, along with my son, my mother-in-law.

Q: *The feeling of loss or nostalgia has therefore more to do with people who are dear to you, to your roots?*
T: I am reminded of the words of a simple person who said, "the man who can't bear to be alone faces death"; this is the sign of a lack of spirituality. This isn't to say that I have no fear of being alone, nor that I consider myself at a higher level of spirituality.

Q: *The regard you have for these photographs is what—love?*
T: Yes, certainly. But I'm not sure that this is a good thing. I rather feel it's a fault, a feeling that weakens me. But perhaps my weakness is my

strength? We know so little about the soul, we're like lost dogs. We feel comfortable when we're speaking of politics, art, sports, love of women. As soon as we touch upon spirituality we lose our way, we're no longer cultured, we lack any preparation in this domain. We're no longer civilized. We become like men who don't know how to clean their teeth. If we come back to *Nostalghia*, one could say this film expresses the nostalgia of spirituality. For example, the concept of victim, we can no longer relate it to ourselves, it exists only for others. We've forgotten what it means to be a victim. It's the reason why the argument of my film is grounded principally on the problem of the victim, less through its subject than through its unfolding.

Q: *When you speak of the soul, do you mean it as a kind of sculpture which a man should secretly accomplish during his life?*
T: Man doesn't have to construct it, but rather liberate it. It is already constructed.

Q: *One last question, which animal would you want to be?*
T: It's difficult to imagine wanting to be an animal, it would be necessary to want to descend spiritually lower, the soul would need to be paralyzed. I'd want to be the animal least dependent upon man. The existence of such an animal is strange to imagine. I don't care for any kind of romanticism, which is why I can't tell you I'd wish to be an eagle or a tiger. Perhaps I'd like to be an animal that caused the least harm possible. Our dog, Dark, is very human, he understands words, he truly feels human emotions. I fear that the dog suffers on account of this. When I had to leave Russia, he sat motionless, he no longer even looked at me.

Between Two Worlds

J. HOBERMAN AND
GIDEON BACHMANN/1983

WHO IS ANDREI TARKOVSKY? Here is a director as ram-
pantly pictorial as Akira Kurosawa, as torturedly moody as
Michelangelo Antonioni, as perversely self-willed as Robert Bresson, as
steeped in his national mythology as John Ford. To American (but not
only American) eyes, the films of the fifty-one-year-old director who
appears to be the Soviet Union's greatest working filmmaker are puz-
zling visions from an enigmatic empire of contradictory signs.

Tarkovsky labors at a Bressonian pace (six features in twenty-one
years). "I agree with Gogol that art should never teach, but show life as
it is," he tells interviewers. Art is "offering one's experiences to one's
contemporaries to judge." The son of a well-known poet, Tarkovsky
studied Arabic and music, painted, and went prospecting in Siberia
before entering the State Institute for Cinema in 1956, where he trained
with the veteran director Mikhail Romm.

The Steamroller and the Violin, Tarkovsky's presciently titled gradua-
tion film—made in 1960 with Andrei Konchalovsky, the future director
of *Siberiade*—attracted considerable attention. His first feature, *Ivan's
Childhood*, was an international success, winning the Best Film Award at
the 1962 Venice Film Festival. Released in the United States the following year as "cultural exchange," under the title *My Name Is Ivan*, the
film's expressionistic blend of dreams, flashbacks, newsreels, and
narrative possibilities in the service of a powerful World War II narrative

---

From *American Film*, November 1983, 14, 75–79. Reprinted by permission of authors.

garnered cautious raves (although one well-known critic complained that the projectionist had surely scrambled the reels).

Ivan was produced during the Khrushchev thaw; Tarkovsky's ambitious second feature, *Andrei Roublev* (co-scripted by Konchalovsky), ran aground in the political turmoil that followed Khrushchev's fall. A Soviet *Lust for Life*, this epic, largely invented biography of Russia's greatest icon painter—set against the carnage of the fifteenth-century Tatar invasions—was historical filmmaking of an audacity unseen in the Soviet Union since Eisenstein's *Ivan the Terrible*. *Roublev* was too violent, too nonlinear, too sexy—and too politically complicated. After a single screening in Moscow (the Dom Kino supposedly ringed with mounted police), the film was shelved.

Tarkovsky declines to speculate why *Roublev* was banned, but he insists he refused to make many of the suggested changes in the film. It was scheduled for the 1968 Cannes Film Festival, then yanked by the Russians at the last minute. The following year it was shown out of competition at Cannes, before opening—with sensational illegality—in Paris. Ultimately, the Soviet cultural bureaucracy relented, releasing the film domestically in 1971. Two years later, *Roublev* surfaced at the New York Film Festival, cut twenty minutes by its American distributor, Columbia Pictures. Most New York reviewers begged off explicating the film, citing its apparent truncation.

Tarkovsky's third feature, *Solaris*, adapted from a distinguished novel by the best-selling Polish science-fiction writer Stanislaw Lem, was again controversial. Lem, dissatisfied with the script, at one point threatened to withdraw his approval and abort the project. Tarkovsky considers the film his weakest. Nevertheless, *Solaris* won a Special Jury Prize at Cannes in 1972, and was hailed as the Soviet *2001*.

Solaris maintains Lem's wonderful premise (a planet consisting entirely of a single, apparently sentient ocean), but jettisons the Pole's characteristically sardonic metaphysics. Within Lem's complex framework one senses another movie struggling to be born. That film, perhaps, is Tarkovsky's *The Mirror*—a work far more suggestive of Stan Brakhage than Stanley Kubrick—released in the Soviet Union in 1974 and in the United States nearly a decade later.

Several years ago, the former editor of this journal asked me what I thought Brakhage might accomplish with a budget the size of Bob

Fosse's for *All That Jazz*. Had I seen *The Mirror*, I would have had a clue: Tarkovsky's mid-career autobiography uses a two-tiered time frame to blend dream sequences and sound footage, childhood memories and scenes from an ongoing marriage with the jolting fluidity of Brakhage's *Sincerity*—another ambivalent celebration of family—which was produced in Colorado at virtually the same time. *The Mirror* received extremely limited distribution in the Soviet Union but extensive criticism from cultural authorities and even Tarkovsky's colleagues. Analyzing their remarks in a 1981 *Film Quarterly*, Michael Dempsey observed that "they all sound amazingly like baby moguls in Hollywood scratching their heads over this artsy wacko who, if you can believe it, doesn't like money."

Yet if Tarkovsky is regarded in Moscow with a wary respect and a latent annoyance that could easily turn ugly, he was nevertheless able to reshoot his next film, *Stalker*, virtually from scratch when a laboratory accident reportedly destroyed the original negative. In the 1979 release, Tarkovsky freely transformed Arkady and Boris Strugatsky's sci-fi novel *Roadside Picnic* into a mock-epic odyssey of two Russian intellectuals led by a tormented fool with the shaven head and dirty rags of a gulag inmate to the mysterious energy source of polluted, post-apocalyptic industrial wasteland.

Tarkovsky's politics are as resistant to easy cold war interpretation as his movies are to genre classification. Like Brakhage or Hans-Jürgen Syberberg, he seems as conservative as he is avant-garde. Indeed, these three strongly individualistic filmmakers form an unholy postwar troika. All are seers who see their art—and all of Art—as a quasi-religious calling; all three tend toward the solipsistic, invoking their parents, mates, and offspring as talismanic elements in their films. All three are natural surrealists, seemingly innocent of official surrealism's radical social program. All three privilege childhood innocence (Syberberg being the most shocking in this case, having spent his childhood in Nazi Germany), and all three are militantly provincial. Tarkovsky is as hopelessly Russian as Syberberg is terminally German and Brakhage totally American. "A forest described in a Japanese book has nothing to do with a forest in Sicily or Siberia," Tarkovsky has said. "I could never see the forest in the same way the author or his countrymen do."

His new film, *Nostalghia*—a brooding account of a journey through Italy, which had its American premiere at last month's New York Film Festival—is the first movie he has made outside the Soviet Union and his most personal since *The Mirror*. In the spectacularly hallucinated ruins of Tuscany, the director confronts his own Russianness. *Nostalghia*, according to Tarkovsky, is virtual psychodrama. The film, he told an Italian journalist, is "about the state of the soul and the feeling of a Soviet intellectual in a foreign land; that is to say, my own condition at this moment."

Some compare Tarkovsky's religious temperament, fervent nationalism, and oceanic yearnings to those of the exiled writer Alexander Solzhenitsyn. Yet as personal as Tarkovsky's films are, he attributes their existence to socialism (or at least state patronage). *The Mirror* and *Stalker*, he told Variety, "would never have been produced outside the Soviet Union—certainly not in Italy or many Western countries where the main objective seems to be a profitable return on a financial investment."

The following remarks by Andrei Tarkovsky have been condensed from more than twenty years of conversations with him by Gideon Bachmann, a freelance journalist and documentary filmmaker.

—J. Hoberman

I have been to Italy quite a few times, and about three years ago I decided, together with my friend the Italian poet, writer, and scriptwriter Tonino Guerra, to make a film called *Nostalghia* about the various experiences I had during these visits.

The main character, Gortchakov, played by Oleg Yankovsky, is a Russian intellectual who is coming to Italy on business. The title, for which "nostalgia" is only a limited translation, means the longing for the faraway, for the worlds that cannot be united, but also for an inner home. The "action" of the film—the story of what happens—was changed again and again during the preparation, during the writing of the script with Guerra, and even while we were shooting. I wanted to express the impossibility of living in a world which is divided, torn apart. Gortchakov is a professor of history, internationally known as an expert of Italian architectural history. It is the first time he has had the chance to see and to touch the monuments and buildings which heretofore he knew and taught only through reproductions and photographs. As soon as he is in Italy, he begins to understand that you cannot transmit, translate, or even just know a work of art if you do not belong to the culture from which it sprang.

But in the larger sense the film is meant to show that you can neither import nor export culture. We, in the Soviet Union, pretend to know Dante and Petrarch, but that is not true. And the Italians pretend to know Pushkin, which cannot really be maintained. Without something very basic happening, it will never be possible to bring to a person the culture of another people.

I do not believe it is my job to attract the public, to get it interested. That would mean that I do not cherish their intelligence. After all, I don't think the public consists of idiots. But I often think of the fact that no producer would spend fifteen kopecks if all I promised to make was a work of art. So I make every film with my full energy and with full engagement as well as I can make it, because, otherwise, I may never be given the opportunity to make another.

In any case, I do not consider it essential to be understood by all. If film is an art form—and I think we all agree that it can be—we mustn't forget that masterpieces are not consumer products but climaxes which express the ideals of an epoch, both from the standpoint of creativity and of the culture from which they derive.

Unfortunately, one cannot often claim that the films one sees go much beyond sheer entertainment. If I appreciate the work of Dovzhenko, Olmi, and Bresson, it is because I am attracted by the simple and the ascetic. I believe these are qualities art should strive for. And faith. Actually, the only way a creative idea can take to reach the consciousness of viewers is by way of the total faith of the creator in the viewer. It must be a sort of discussion between them on an equal level. There is no other way. Many parts of the modern film serve no other purpose than that of explaining to the viewer the circumstances of the film's action. In the cinema one need not explain, but one must directly affect the emotions. The awakened emotion then moves thoughts forward.

I am seeking a principle of montage which would permit me to show the subjective logic—the thought, the dream, the memory—instead of the logic of the subject. I am looking for a form which derives from the situation and the psychic condition of man—that is, from the factors that affect human behavior. This is the first condition for the presentation of psychological truth. Thus, in my films, the story is never of great importance. The real significance of my works has never been expressed through actions. I try to speak of what is most important, without interference. To show things which are not necessarily linked logically. It is the movement of thoughts which makes them join together inwardly.

Only one kind of journey is possible: the one we undertake to our inside world. From running about on the surface of the planet, we don't learn much. Nor do I believe that one travels in order to return. Man can never return to his point of departure, because he himself, in the meantime, changes. And, of course, you can't escape from yourself; what you are, you carry with you. We carry the house of our souls like the tortoise its shell. To travel the countries of the world is only symbolically a journey. Wherever you get to, you are still seeking your own soul.

I see the only meaning of human existence in the effort to overcome yourself spiritually, to become different from what you are at birth, in growing. If in that span, between the poles of birth and death, we manage to achieve this—even if it is hard and the advance is small—we will have served humanity.

I am ever more interested in Oriental philosophies, in which the sense of existence lies in contemplation and in the fusion of man and universe. The West is too rational and the sense of Western existence seems to be rooted in a pragmatic principle: a little bit of everything in perfect equilibrium in order to keep one's own body alive as long as possible.

It appears to me that mankind has stopped believing in itself. That is, not "mankind"—such a thing does not exist–but each person for himself. When I think of today's man, I see him like a singer in a choir opening and closing his mouth in rhythm with the singing, but producing no tone. After all, the others are all singing! He just pretends to sing along, since he is convinced that the voices of the others suffice. He behaves this way because he no longer believes in the importance of his own, personal actions—a man without faith, totally without hope of influencing through his own behavior the society in which he lives.

I am convinced that "time" is no objective category, since time cannot exist without man. Certain scientific discoveries tend to reach the same conclusion. We do not live in the "now." The now is so short, so close to zero without being zero, that we have no way of perceiving it. The moment which we call "now" immediately becomes past, and what we call future becomes present and then at once it becomes past. The only possible present is our fall into the abyss which exists between future and present. That's why "nostalgia" is not regret for the past but sadness for the lost span during which we did not manage to count our forces, to marshal them, and to do our duty.

The nostalgia of my film is a fatal illness suffered by someone who is far from his own origins and cannot return there. But in film, things are not so linear; it is important to remember that no character has the right to speak directly for the author or to express, in a linear way, the author's ideas. For example, whatever my main character's view of women may be, they are not necessarily my ideas about women. For my part, I certainly do not go around raving about the feminist movement, but I respect the woman in women. There is no doubt that women are human beings like men, but their function and role in human existence is quite different from the function and role of men.

And it is not only wrong to forget this, but it's going against nature to do so. We have become very good at this, in fact: doing things that are against nature. In our attempts to protect ourselves from nature and to conquer it, we have given so much preference to our material development that we've ended up quite unprepared to cope with the technology we have created . To me, man, in his substance, is essentially a spiritual being and the meaning of his life consists in developing this spirituality. If he fails to do so, society deteriorates.

Quite unexpectedly to me, *Nostalghia* conveyed my own state of mind about this conflict between spirit and matter. More than that: For the first time, I suddenly felt that the cinema is capable of going a long way toward expressing the author's spiritual state. I had not expected to be capable of such clear embodiment in a film.

These realizations became possible because I cut the entire picture after I had finished shooting, something I had never done in Russia, where I had always edited as I went along. This had made it possible to prepare the next lot of filming, to clear up anything that had gone wrong, or to change things; in a word, the whole time I was filming I was dependent on the impressions of what had been filmed previously. In filming *Nostalghia*, this did not happen, and at first it was hard for me. But something else became possible this way: The material of the film can be seen very much as a whole and there is one level of emotional intensity throughout.

My discovery was just this: that it had in fact been the same thing that I had been concerned with all these years. That's what was sudden and unexpected: that while the films may have been different, they had been made for the same reason—to discuss man's inner conflict resulting from the ambiguous position he finds himself in, between some kind of spiritual ideal and the necessity of existing in this material world. I consider this conflict fundamental, since it gives rise to all the problems in contemporary society. Let's call it "the Tolstoy complex." It's eternal, and will also be at the base of the *Hamlet* I am planning to make in a contemporary setting.

Ever since art has existed, mankind has always strived to influence the world through it. But on the whole it has always failed to have much social or political effect. I think now, looking around me and also looking back, art cannot really affect social development. It can only influence the development of minds. It can work on our intelligence and on our spirit. But for changing things, there are greater social forces than art. After all, practically all human endeavor has as its aim the changing of the world.

And, in fact, the face of things changes continually. But why, I ask you, if man has been changing the face of the world for centuries through his works, has it reached this appalling state? Maybe we haven't been ready for it?

It seems to me that before trying to alter the world, man needs to alter himself; he needs to change his spiritual existence, his own inner world, quietly, harmoniously, in synchronicity with his other activities. Our greatest crime, perhaps, is the attempt to change others, to instruct, to try to "change the world through art," without having undertaken transformations upon ourselves. The social function of art can only be a second step.

In any case, I agree with Gogol that art should never teach, but show life as it is, in the extended sense—offer one's experiences to one's contemporaries to judge. To be allowed to go beyond this—to make art "useful," as if one were a prophet–you must gain this right to do so by first becoming sufficiently aware spiritually. And maybe one can never gain this right, never be *sufficiently* aware. All we can do as artists is, I keep repeating, to attract man's attention to the problems of existence. When things are going well, people can get along without artists.

My Cinema in a Time of Television

VELIA IACOVINO/1983

IT ISN'T ALWAYS POSSIBLE to establish a contact with others through words. Sometimes, one creates a direct bond, beyond language, emotional and wholly irrational, through which it is possible to communicate solely with a glance, a smile, with a slight movement of the hand. Something similar to this occurred with Andrei Tarkovsky, perhaps the most important Russian director of our time, when I interviewed him in Rome for *MassMedia*. It was a captivating and unforgettable moment. Small, slight, he looked around and moved with his somewhat Tatar features contracted into a scowl. He asked me to show him the magazine. He leafed through *MassMedia* pausing to read one or two of the headlines. Then he recomposed himself. He smiled, and his Asiatic eyes finally stopped sending out imperceptible sparks of discomfort. "I'm ready," he said, after a silent pause, in his somewhat comical Italian. And turning to an interpreter friend, he began to answer my questions.

Q: *Mr. Tarkovsky, in your opinion, is film passing through a difficult moment, as difficult as the passing from silent to sound film?*
T: Of course. I'd say that film is passing through a moment that is far more difficult and critical than the one that marked the beginning of sound in film. A moment that I don't quite know how to deal with. And this has not happened because of the use of new technologies, but strictly because of economic pressures and motivations. The fact is that

From *MassMedia*, no. 5 (November–December 1983). Reprinted by permission. Translated from Italian by Ken Shulman.

in truth, film is now in the hands of big producers. American producers. And these producers are primarily interested in getting videocassettes out into the market. They want to realize ever higher profits, instead of trying to satisfy the tastes of that large segment of the public which has become more intelligent, and, as a consequence, more demanding. We're talking about big business here. That's the story. We're talking about a mechanism that will be very difficult to dismantle or slow down, even in the name of artistic quality.

Q: *Do you think there is such a thing as a national cinematic language? Or is it true instead that a Swiss director has the same cinematic language and the same technique as a Canadian or Soviet director?*
T: If cinema is an art, it naturally has a national language. Art cannot keep from being national. In short, Russian cinema is Russian, and Italian cinema is Italian.

Q: *In 1976, you directed* Hamlet *on stage, and achieved enormous success. Is directing for the stage very different than directing for film?*
T: Theater and cinema are two different art forms. Two different professions. To realize a theatrical show, for example, you need to have a theater at your disposal, in which you can train the company and prepare your actors. But this, it seems, is not always possible. However, apart from the difference in the location where the action takes place, that which you can do in theater you cannot do in cinema. And vice versa. I think, however, that all art forms, even if they are different, are in the end equivalent. They have the same worth and weight, and have the same effect on reality.

Q: *Do you think cinema has eclipsed theater?*
T: No, I don't believe so. They are two things, as I've already said, that are completely different.

Q: *What changes when instead of shooting a film for the big screen you shoot it for television?*
T: When you make a film, you have to be constantly aware whether you are making it for the big screen or for television. Because the spectators' mode of perception will change completely, depending on whether

they are immersed in the dark, crowded hall, or home, alone, with their remote control, amidst an infinity of possible distractions. Furthermore, going to the cinema is an act of volition. Watching a film on television isn't always that. Often you suffer or endure the image on television, an image which acts subliminally, even changing people's tastes.

Q: *Don't you believe that seeing too many films—as can happen with many television spectators—can cause a dangerous flight into fantasy?*
T: Television certainly has a strong influence on the psychology of those who watch it. I'm convinced that it can also modify taste. But I don't think it can seduce or alter spectators to a point where they lose touch with reality.

Q: *In what way is the medium of television transforming the public's tastes?*
T: Since the public started watching television consistently, it goes to the cinema with a different spirit. It no longer goes to the cinema just to be distracted or for entertainment. It goes to see something that it is worth seeing, something completely new.

Q: *What has television taken from cinema? And what has it given?*
T: Television hasn't taken anything from cinema. On the contrary, I believe that television has a greater influence on film than film does on television, in that it stimulates cinema to seek higher quality. In addition, television is a means of information we truly can't do without. It has become indispensable, even if the enormous quantity of news it broadcasts is often superficial and only serves to confuse people.

Q: *In the past, you've stated that cinema is a means of ideological education for the masses. Do you still believe this?*
T: Certainly. I haven't changed my opinion. Rather, I'd like to add that all art forms, and not just cinema, should have as their aim to shape the organic man of the future.

Q: *Your cinema has been defined "a poetic cinema." Do you agree?*
T: Critics say that I'm a poet. Every art form can be poetry. All the greatest musicians, writers, and painters are also great poets.

Q: *In your opinion, is poetry the expression of beauty for beauty's sake? Or is it a means to confront and alter reality?*

T: Poetry doesn't alter reality. It creates it.

Q: *Mr. Tarkovsky, do you believe that it's easier for art to exist without power, or for power to exist without art?*

T: Art is not made out of power. Art is made by artists.

Q: *What is, for you, the specific power of film?*

T: Unlike all the other art forms, film is able to seize and render the passage of time, to stop it, almost to possess it in infinity. I'd say that film is the sculpting of time.

Q: *For Fellini, cinema was "a mirror, a window, a way to continue dreaming, to look inside yourself." What is cinema for you? What does it represent?*

T: I don't agree with Fellini. Cinema is not a way to continue dreaming. Nor is it an art through which we try to mirror reality as it is, or to deform it and reflect a grotesque image. For me, cinema is simply an original way to create a new universe, a fascinating world that we show to others so they can discover all its hidden wonders.

Q: *Is it fair to say "this is a film by Tarkovsky"? Or is it also obligatory that we speak of the actors, the screenwriters, the cameramen, and the others?*

T: Of course it's not only the director or the actors who work on a film. A film doesn't belong 100 percent to the director. Nor does it belong to the actors. It belongs to all those who contributed to its production.

Q: *Can you tell us why the release of* Andrei Roublev *was delayed so long in the Soviet Union?*

T: I don't know the reasons. And I ignore them. I only know that initially they decided to screen the film at the Cannes Film Festival and that, instead, they suddenly changed their minds. The film was detained. Evidently something happened, something I really can't explain.

Q: *In your opinion, is there a difference between directing in the USSR and directing in the West?*

T: There were people who had scared me about this. They told me it was very difficult to work in the West. But I didn't find a great difference.

Actually, I think it's the opposite. Certainly, here, it's like running a race against yourself every day, when you make a film and you immediately think of the money involved. This, I have to say, didn't happen in the USSR.

Q: *Is it fair to represent the figure of Andrei Roublev as a metaphor for the artist who assumes the responsibility of opening the eyes of the public, of those who neither hear nor speak, who are represented in the figure of the deaf-mute?*
T: In this film the artist is only the spokesperson of the masses. He expresses the ideas of the masses, those ideas that the masses frequently perceive, in a confused manner, and are not able to organize or express.

Q: *In your films, the camera often pauses on water, on fire, on snow, on horses. Why? Are these elements perhaps used symbolically?*
T: No, they're not symbols. They are manifestations of that nature in which we live.

Q: *Then what meaning has the water that runs down the icon at the end of* Andrei Roublev?
T: It's difficult for me to explain. In this case I used water because it is a vital, living substance, that continually changes form, that moves. It's a very cinematographic element. And through this I tried to express an idea of the passage of time. Of the movement of time.

Q: *Some say that your film* Solaris *was significantly changed when it was dubbed into Italian.*
T: In its Italian version, my film was essentially destroyed. The montage was changed. It was the work of Dacia Maraini. I don't know what part Pasolini might have had in it. But it was an authentic act of barbarism. Among many things, they speak in dialect in this film. It's monstrous. A disaster.

Q: *Where do you place* Nostalghia *in the arc of your career?*
T: *Nostalghia* was a very important film for me. I was able to fully express myself. And I have to say that I received confirmation that

cinema is a great art form, capable of representing even the imperceptible states of the soul.

Q: *Recently you said that the greatest things that man can do are born in silence and solitude. A film is born in quite another manner. Does this mean that in cinema, it's impossible to do great things?*
T: A film is also born in silence and solitude. It begins to take form in that moment when its author first thinks about it.

Q: *Which Italian directors do you prefer?*
T: Antonioni, Fellini, Olmi. The Taviani brothers. And others. They are all full of life. Bellocchio . . .

Q: *What sort of atmosphere did you find at the Cannes Film Festival this year?*
T: Some dreadful things happened at Cannes this year. I simply made a film about nostalgia, about melancholy. And it was a bitter pill for me to swallow when Bondarchuk, the Soviet member of the jury, didn't accept my film. Everyone liked it except for him. I'm very offended and I'm surprised that the Soviet leaders permitted such an opinion to prevail on such a patriotic film.

Q: *Which is the film for which you feel the greatest affection?*
T: I love all of my films. I don't know how to answer. Perhaps I feel closest to *Nostalghia*. It's the last. In it I find myself.

Q: *What emotions can best be represented through film?*
T: You can express all emotions through film. It's an art form, like all the others. It depends on the intentions of the director.

Q: *Does it still make sense to make film in black and white?*
T: Without a doubt. Black and white film is able to better represent the essence of reality, to express intrinsic meaning. This doesn't happen with color. I'd say that film in color is more common, more vulgar.

Q: *What are your plans for the future? Can you give us a few peeks?*
T: Donatella Baglivo has just finished a television special on my work as a director. It's not exactly a film. It's more of how *Nostalghia* was

made. It's interesting and very original. For my part I'm planning to stage "Boris Godunov" at Covent Garden in London, and to make a film version of *Hamlet*. But for the moment I'm waiting for my country to send me permission for this work sojourn. I'm also waiting for them to send my son and his grandmother. I should be abroad for three years.

An Enemy of Symbolism

IRENA BREZNA/1984

Q: *Andrei Tarkovsky, in the USSR you are a privileged artist . . .*
T: I believe this impression is wrong. I am not privileged there. The
film director, Bondarchuk, for example, is privileged, but not I.

Q: *But you are famous and that probably is to your advantage, maybe also
to your disadvantage.*
T: This fame, this popularity, I do not sense it; I am not interested in
it. I was never occupied with my fame. It has no meaning for me.

Q: *Doesn't it give you more possibilities to work without compromise?*
T: Certainly. It is important to the artist to realize that his work has
not failed. That gives him a certain satisfaction. The fact that the Soviet,
the English, and specifically, the German public is giving me a lot of
attention, confirms this for me. It has no special advantages for me; it
only reassures me that I am right in doing my work. It is reassuring and
raises my self-confidence, but fundamentally it has no meaning for me.

Q: *It seems to me that you are annoyed by the spotlight. You try to avoid
public contact. For example, you seldom give interviews.*
T: Yes, I am not a sociable person. There are people who take advantage of fame, and who enjoy contact with journalists. I don't like it at
all. I have not yet been satisfied by an article that has come out after a
conversation with a journalist. Not because I was not complimented,

From *Tip*, March 1984. Reprinted by permission. Translated from German by Zsuzsanna Pál.

but because the articles are not concerned with what has been discussed. It is a burden for me to sense that I have become a subject of interest to someone because of my fame. It makes me angry.

Q: *What is it that makes you angry?*
T: It is hard to answer. I feel that people who get together to talk should have something in common, so that the conversation doesn't get one-sided. When the journalist poses his question, he is not interested in the answer, but in his notes. The conversation doesn't move him, it only has meaning for his work. In the same way, the film viewer as conversation partner angers me, because of his curiosity about me. In short, such conversations are not genuine and that makes me furious. People socialize but there is no mutual, genuine interest; they meet in a round-about way.

Q: *And you wish for genuine contact?*
T: Everyone is wishing for that to a certain degree, it seems to me. There is a great deal of ingenuousness in many things we do, especially in public, a lot of nothingness and nonsense. I do not see any sense in such conversations unless I myself find it important to say something. Since I make films, I try to say everything in my work.

Q: *You would like to make it clear to me that the basis for our conversation is quite negative?*
T: It is always like this. There is nothing to be done about it. What does that mean anyway, a negative basis? We don't have a basis. There is only your wish to interview me and my wish to resist you with all my power.

Q: *I can strongly sense that.*
T: Now let's see how our conversation continues: I think it was Goethe who said, "If you want an intelligent answer, ask an intelligent question."

Q: *Mr. Tarkovsky, you are mistaken if you think we have nothing in common. I came to you because I feel close to you through your films. This interview is only a pretext for me to be able to speak to you.*
T: This you will have to prove to me.

Q: *I hope I will be able to. It is because of you that I came to London. That an article will come out of it is only secondary, but it comes with it.*
T: I see, you would like to connect everything.

Q: *First, it was my wish to meet you. Then, I came upon all these hindrances in order to be able to do so.*
T: Unfortunately, you overcame them all. I had hoped that you, like all other journalists, would stumble over these hindrances, but you are here.

Q: *I besieged and conquered you like a fortress. Now I am here and I don't know how to speak to you.*
T: Speak normally.

Q: *Listen, I am deeply touched by your films; your view of things seems so familiar, except that I can't see myself in them as a woman. Women play an absolutely traditional role in your films. The male world dominates, or better, there is only the male world. The woman is mysterious from the male point of view. She is loving; loving the man, her whole existence revolves around her relationship with the man. The woman doesn't have a life of her own.*
T: I have never thought about that, I mean about the woman's interior world. It would be difficult to deny the woman her own world, but it seems to me that this world is very strongly connected to the world of the man that the woman is involved with. From this point of view, a solitary woman is an abnormality.

Q: *And a solitary man, is that normal?*
T: It is more normal than a non-solitary man. That is why the woman is either completely missing in my films or she is created through the power of the man. The woman only exists in two of my films, in *The Mirror* and in *Solaris*. And there it is obvious that she depends on the man. Do you reject this role of the woman?

Q: *How could I accept it? I, for my part, can't see myself in it.*
T: So you find that the man you live with should make his world dependent on yours?

Q: *Not at all. I keep my world, and he keeps his.*

T: That is impossible. If you keep your world, and he keeps his, you will have nothing in common. The inner world has to become a common one. If not, the relationship has no future, it is hopeless, unharmonious, and bound to die. When a woman changes partners, I tend to find that odd. The concern is not how many men she has had; I am concerned with the principle. The thing is, that the woman experiences these marriages like illnesses. That means that first she suffers one illness then another one and so forth. Love is such a total feeling that it can't be repeated, regardless of the form it takes; it is unrepeatable in its totality. When and if the woman can repeat this feeling, it is completely meaningless to her. It could be that this woman has been without luck or that she always tried to keep her own world, that she found her world more important and was afraid to dissolve into a foreign world. But then she can't count on being taken seriously. Do you understand?

Q: *Have you never met a woman who has her own world?*

T: I can't relate to such a woman.

Q: *You yourself never would dissolve into a woman, if I understand you correctly?*

T: No, I don't dissolve. I don't need that. I am a man.

Q: *But you need a woman who dissolves into you?*

T: Naturally. If a woman tries to keep her self, then the relationship is cold.

Q: *But you preserve yourself in this love.*

T: I am a man. I am of a different nature.

Q: *Do you have the impression that you know the female nature?*

T: I have an opinion about it, like you.

Q: *But I recognize myself as a woman from the inside, because I am a woman.*

T: People can judge themselves least of all. The woman who wants to preserve her own world surprises me. It seems to me that the woman's meaning, the meaning of female love, is self-sacrifice. That is the woman's greatness. I bow before such a woman. I know such cases.

Q: *There is no shortage of such cases in the world.*
T: Yes, those were great women. I don't know a single woman who insists on her own world and so proves her greatness. Name just one.

Q: *I am speechless. So the woman only has the right to exist in her love for the man?*
T: Did I say that? We only talked about the male-female relationship. And I was not able to express something without having my assertiveness attacked.

Q: *You have already said enough, you know very well.*
T: I only said that it is impossible for a person, when he or she loves, to keep a confined world of his or her own, because this world melts with that of the other into something completely different. If one frees the woman from this relationship, one destroys the relationship. The woman can't get up, shake off everything, and five minutes later begin a new life. The woman's inner world depends on her feelings toward the man. In my opinion, she has to, absolutely must be dependent on them. The woman is the symbol of love. Love is Man's greatest possession, in the materialistic as well as the spiritual sense of the word. And the woman gives the meaning of life. It is not a coincidence that the Virgin Mary is a symbol of love, as the virgin who bore the Savior. When I speak to women about this subject, they always talk about the feeling of dignity that one seemingly wants to rob them of. From my point of view, these women don't understand that they only find their dignity in a male-female relationship in total devotion to the man. When the woman really loves, then she doesn't keep track, then she doesn't ask questions like you. She wouldn't know what you are talking about.

Q: *I wonder why you ask for total love from someone else, especially a woman. Why can't you devote yourself to love and leave it to the woman to do what she has to do?*
T: That would, of course, be possible. I don't ask for a certain behavior from anyone. I am only saying that the woman, in order to express her

whole spiritual self, should not insist on her own world at that
moment. Otherwise, the following happens: "Please keep your world,
I keep mine . . . and good-bye."

Q: *You don't believe that two equal individuals can give more to each
other? What do you expect when the woman stops existing as a personality
and only lives through you? What do you get from it?*
T: I can comprehend her inner world and I open my world to her.
If the woman remains in her world we will never recognize each
other.

Q: *From a logical point of view, if the woman's world dissolves into yours,
her world would not be understandable to you. She wouldn't have a world of
her own. Only your world becomes larger.*
T: Why do you think this? And why couldn't it be the other way
around? I would be very interested in that. If you acknowledge this is
one case, why do you deny it in another?

Q: *I am of the opinion that I can love and have my own world at the same
time. And I have to have it. It is absolutely necessary. I find that the woman's
total devotion to the man which you are talking about bears a great danger
for the woman. If the woman chooses to live through the man, she is in danger of ending up empty-handed. This is an old, a very old story. I know it very
well. I myself occasionally have a strong tendency to dissolve into love.*
T: Thank God. Be proud of it. And don't think that I demand this
"dissolving" from the woman. Unfortunately for myself, I only seldom
have this feeling of love. It happens very seldom, and when it does
one can only envy the person, man or woman. When I talk about it, it
doesn't mean that I require devotion from anyone. These things are
impossible to demand. Love can't be enforced by power. So my point of
view isn't dangerous to anyone.

Q: *Love either happens or it doesn't?*
T: Yes, it happens or it doesn't. When it doesn't, nothing happens and
Man slowly dies. This is only my opinion. Naturally, there are relationships where people, everyone for himself, become more and more independent and that means they become colder to each other, more

egotistical. Maybe it is easier this way. Such relationships are, of course, less dangerous, comfortable. And they move somewhere on the level of feminism. The meaning of feminism, to me, is not only to secure social rights for women. Although the woman's social situation today is not dramatic in the way it used to be, and in a few years the balance will have been reached. Strange, very strange, these women who, speaking about this, insist on their similarities with men and don't understand their uniqueness as women. This has always astonished me, because the woman's inner world is fundamentally very different from that of the man. I believe that the woman can't exist independent of the man because of her specialness. If she exists independently from the man, she is no longer natural, organic. She certainly is able to hold a position in society; she can do a man's work, but does that make her a woman? No, never. Some women think, by doing a man's job, they become equal. But a woman doesn't need to ask for the same rights as a man. The woman is totally different from the man. She has a uniqueness, something important, something fundamental that the man is missing. Women are looking for equal rights. I understand what they mean; they don't want the self-sacrifice anymore. They find that they have always been suppressed, and they believe that they can free themselves through equal rights. They don't understand that everyone, man or woman, is free if he or she wants to be free naturally. We all are free human beings, but not because we might live in a free country. That is not an important reason. The stonemason of ancient Rome might have been within a free man . . . Man is basically free. If he isn't, it is his, and only his, fault. Of course, it is hard to be free. Finally we have arrived at the essence of the matter. It always makes me angry when people blame everybody else for not being able to live. When one tells me one is unfree, that makes me furious. If you want to be free, be free. Who is hindering you? If you want to be happy, but you are unhappy, be happy. We patronize others with a lot of enthusiasm and a waste of energy. And we, ourselves, are not able to behave accordingly. When someone is vehemently fighting against something, I understand that this person should start looking within himself. I don't deny the fact that women have largely been excluded from the events of the world. Undoubtedly, this is unjustified. But I don't know yet what will happen to the woman when she will be completely integrated into public life.

I would like to emphasize that I am not against this, *I am for it,* but I have the impression that she will not find herself there. She will not find satisfaction.

Q: *I agree with you. As long as male values dominate, it will be hard for a woman in this world, as long as she has to compete with male values in her career.*

T: You are mistaken. For me there is nothing more unpleasant than a woman with a big career. Not because I fear for my male rights, but because I see it as something unnatural. There is a woman taking a route that she should have ignored. Only a misleading, competitive feeling for the man has caused her to do it. And why does this happen? Does the woman want to be like the man? Does she want to prove her similar abilities to the man? I don't doubt that a woman can fulfill a man's job. Here in England a woman has fought her way to a big political career and is one of the toughest politicians. As a politician she behaves correctly. She is in conflict with a lot of people, but for a politician that is a good sign. A politician who pleases is a bad one. A politician has to accomplish something and that makes him unpopular. During the Falkland conflict one could dislike this woman, but her point of view concerning the Grenada invasion was understandable. A woman's ability to do a man's job is nothing special. Of course she can do it. But that doesn't prove anything.

Q: *One can understand Margaret Thatcher. It is not astonishing when a woman has to adopt male values in a male domain. There is nothing else she can do. She doesn't have a choice. What troubles me about your statement is your premise of the so-called true nature of women. Because women have lived in a male-dominated world for centuries, it is hard to crystalize what female nature is and how women could create a world with female values.*

T: Excuse me, what is your name?

Q: *Irena.*

T: Listen, Irena, you are already saying that you are not content with your female nature.

Q: *No, you have misunderstood me.*
T: But there couldn't be a different male–female relationship than the one that has always existed, the one that has been created. Because our world is two-gendered, like it or not. Maybe on another planet there is a one or a five-gendered world where that kind of constellation is necessary to secure the continuation of life. Maybe there, there are five genders necessary for physical and spiritual love. But on Earth, two are necessary. For some reason we always forget this. We speak of rights, condition, dependence. We never speak of the fact that a woman is a woman and a man is a man. Your sole objection could be that you don't like it.

Q: *I have difficulties accepting that you always put the woman in a dependent position in relation to the man, and never vice versa, and that you furnish the woman with attributes of love and self-sacrifice for the man, when it seems to be that you, yourself, are thirsting for love and the ability to sacrifice. But for some, to me unknown, reason you don't seem to have the ability to have these feelings.*
T: I don't know. That might be. I can't judge that. I have a hard time constructing sentences like you do.

Q: *Femininity for me doesn't lie in dependence on another person, and so I can't find myself in your film heroines. All those women are satellites gravitating to the planet Man, without the slightest possibility for self-dynamism.*
T: This is strange. I have received a lot of letters from women, back in Moscow, by the way, who told me that I had succeeded in my movie *The Mirror* in opening up and penetrating their world which they had believed to be inaccessible and opaque to the rest of the world. Maybe you have a different personality structure. You have different demands for yourself. Obviously, you are not like the mother in *The Mirror*. *The Mirror* is about my mother. It is not fiction; it is based on reality. There is not a single fictive episode in it. Maybe you are right and you haven't found yourself there.

Q: *The basic human condition and your treatment of it, especially in* Stalker *and* Solaris *has touched me very much. This is the reason I am here.*

Also the way you portray love in Solaris *is grand and subtle. But love is Hari's sole power and at the same time her Achilles' heel. She only has love.*

T: And you don't want an Achilles' heel. You want to be invulnerable.

Q: *A woman often finds herself in a dilemma of having to choose between love and her own personality. The man has the only possible way from the beginning, that of his personality.*

T: Woman will never conquer man in the male way.

Q: *Only in a perverted society, in our case, a male one, can personality be one-gendered.*

T: Without the total love of the woman, male-female relationships will be different.

Q: *Yes, they will be different; they should be different. Try to imagine for a second to be a woman having been led to live for others for centuries, never for yourself, always being disposable to others. Can you feel the burden?*

T: And you think it is easier for a man?

Q: *Not at all. The way things are now, it is hard for both.*

T: To be a man is as hard as it is to be a woman. The misery is based on something else. We live in a society where Man's spiritual level is very low. And we know that we go to sleep today and might not wake up tomorrow. If some lunatic pushes a button, three bombs will be enough to eliminate life on this planet. Not that we are not conscious of this, but we continually forget. Our spiritual interests are enslaved by materialism to such a degree, that we have to deal with issues that should never have come up. The development of social questions is the result of our insane anti-spiritualism. A spiritually fulfilled woman would never think of feeling enslaved or humiliated in her relationship to the man. Just as a spiritually fulfilled man would never think of demanding something from a woman. Only you, through the power of your argument have brought me to answers like these. It should be foreign to us to talk about such issues. The fact that we talk about it shows that something is not in order. The problem should be a natural thing. But the already achieved or still-to-be

achieved rights for women will not give women self-confirmation. On
the contrary, only then will she feel humiliation. "Why," she will ask
herself, "do I, a human being so different from a man, why do I lead a
man's life?" These problems are signs of our nonspirituality. I have met
astonishing women, astonishing in their spirituality. Those women did
not trouble themselves with such problems, but they had themselves
demonstrated such inner wealth, such spiritual greatness, such moral
strength, that every man would have to fall on his knees and not feel
ashamed, but honored. You see, this is the point. If we start to clarify
our relationships we are already in a bad way. The longing for it is a
symptom of our discontent and not the search for justice. Those are
two completely different categories. I see that women are in a terrible
situation today. A truly loving woman doesn't ask questions like that.
She is not interested in it.

Q: *A truly loving woman doesn't confine her love to a man, but extends it
on to the world. You spoke of the nuclear threat, which was created through
male dominance.*
T: Madame Curie also worked on that.

Q: *We are talking about male values that dominate the world. In a society
where female values would have a strong influence it might not have resulted
in such an apocalyptic threat. How do you envision that a woman today,
knowing about the Apocalypse, would not feel responsible and connected, but
would instead sacrifice herself in total love to a single man, with the perspective that this man, still warm from her love, destroys the planet?*
T: That is shocking, that is shocking. I understand what you are saying. But I am astonished, Irena, you are mistaken if you think that a
man is not troubled by the same feelings and worries. If you believe
that the man is lord on this planet, you are mistaken.

Q: *And who is lord?*
T: He.

Q: *Where is he?*
T: (*points upward*) Do you see the point? We are discussing events,
not reasons. We are talking about the most important thing. If Man

lives without knowing the reason for his existence, without knowing for what reason he was born into this world and why he is to live for some decades, then the world must come to the state in which it is now. Man has, since the Enlightenment, dealt with things he should have ignored. He began to turn toward material things. The thirst for knowledge took over Man, particularly males. Women don't thirst for knowledge as much as men. Fortunately.

Q: *Women maybe have a sensitivity for other perceptions.*
T: Yes, exactly. So you realized that. And what happened? Man started dancing around himself as though he was blind. Except for the hands there was no organ left to perceive the world. We had already perceived so much of this world and one would think that this would be enough to reach happiness and harmony. No, on the contrary. The more we "know about the world," the clearer specialists see that, in reality, we know even less than our ancestors. We are in the power of confusion. If you are blind and touch a cold radiator, you will feel that the world around you is cold or vice versa when the heat is turned on. That doesn't matter. But this realization has no connection to the real world; it only refers to the sense of touching. It is pathetic to think that our perception of the world relies on the fact that the heating is turned on or off. We have decided that we know a lot about the world. We don't know anything. The small part of the world we now have a vague notion of, doesn't give us an overall picture, because the world is infinite. In my opinion the pathos of human existence doesn't lie in comprehension; that is Man's intellectual task, but not the main one. The human problem is to live with the knowledge of the meaning of life. How curious that we perceive the world from a pragmatic, profitable, advantageous side. We keep producing prosthetics. All technologies are based on that. We invented airplanes because we were tired of riding on horseback. We think to enrich our lives by moving faster. That is an elementary mistake, which can be seen with the naked eye. We find new energy by splitting atoms. And how do we use that energy? We produce the atomic bomb, the suicide weapon. I am saying that we are unable to properly use these discoveries. That is because Man doesn't know why he lives. The scientist believes his purpose is to make discoveries. That is a pragmatic approach to the truth. The artist

lives to produce works of art. Everyone lives with particular duties, everyone feels the inequality and is jealous of the other one, when everyone should grasp his one purpose in life and live it. On this ground everyone is right and has equal rights: artists, workers, priests, farmers, children, dogs, men, and women. If this sense of life remains hidden in us, we start to flounder and invent problems that wouldn't exist if we recognized the meaning of life. That is my point of view. If we take it from the beginning, everything stays in its place. The crisis of our civilization developed from a disproportion. Two notions are in disharmony—that of material development and that of spiritual development.

Q: *This began already with Plato.*
T: No, much earlier. It began when man decided to defend himself against nature and other men. Our society developed on this faulty basis. People don't relate to each other in love, in friendship, out of the need for spiritual contact, but from the impulse to take advantage. To survive, naturally. But I believe Man would have survived in any case, because he is human, not animal. We know of examples where Man lived in harmony with nature and achieved astonishing things. For example, those Eastern cultures documented in Sanskrit which were able to achieve a balance between the spiritual and the material world. We still have traces of those cultures, which tell us that civilization once took a different, truer, direction. One may ask why those civilizations died out. It seems that because other cultures evolved parallel to them and they developed some sort of hostility towards each other, those civilizations didn't have any possibility of developing their concepts. The reasons are unknown. In any case, Man should realize that he was born into this world with the purpose of spiritually rising above himself, to overcome what we call evil, the evil which has its source in egotism. Egotism is a symptom of the fact that Man doesn't love himself, that he has an incorrect understanding of the notion of love. This is the source of the deformation of everything. The idiocy of our science, its errors and its devastating results, are not the consequence of the fact that women haven't taken over at the right time, but that Man is not at his highest spiritually. If humanity would move in the direction of spiritual values and wasn't in search of a

source of energy, but a spiritual source, then all this we are talking about would not exist. Then Man would develop harmonically under the control of a spiritual process. I don't think that the spiritual process could produce such a one-sidedness as the intellectual process. Spirituality already includes the notion of harmony. Everything else, as right as you may be, is secondary. If you haven't recognized yourself in my films, that doesn't mean that I was wrong. I have said the truth about the women I wanted to portray. You might dislike it. Or would you like me to portray the woman in the sense of social realism?

Q: *You have prejudices against me.*
T: No, you are wrong; you are the one who has prejudices against me. I think you should ask the man you live with, "Why are you so stupid?" This is how one has to pose the question.

Q: *If this is the cardinal question between me and a man, then there would-n't be time to ask it, because I would be gone before that.*
T: Understandable. You know, we produce these secondary problems, try to solve them and think we can rescue the world which is in crisis. But we are making an error. In my mind, it is very dangerous indeed, to be occupied with questions like that because it is keeping us from the main thing, from the struggle for spirituality. The struggle for spiritual-ity is being fought on all fronts. That is how everyone understands it. Everyone, also an uneducated but spiritually developed person, under-stands the main problem. For example, I lived in a village near Rome. There I met a man who had worked the soil all his life. He told me about the fact that labor in farming is, as we all understand, very important, though it pays less than anything else. "If I would be inter-ested in my own profit," he said, "I would have to leave farming and open a grocery store, for example. Then I would be well off. But I would never do that," said this completely uneducated man. "And why?" I asked. "How could I? I could never let myself," he answered. See, this man has a sense of responsibility. This proves his spirituality. Not for materialistic reasons, but out of love for his work, he stays on the farm or makes sacrifices for the community. In this lies a certain spiritual beauty. He can't leave the soil. And we, certainly sympathetic people,

can leave the land with a calm conscience. This farmer has high ethical standards, this is why I liked him.

Q: *He has respect for the soil.*
T: For the soil, for Man, and first of all for himself. That is most important. He respects himself. He preserves his inner, spiritual world. This is very important. And he has no problems. A man who has a true sense of responsibility toward himself has no basic problems. We want to live, understand the meaning of life, fulfill our responsibilities toward life on this earth, but often we can't achieve this. We are still too weak. But it is important to choose this way. As long as we can't answer this question, it won't let us go. Unfortunately, society today is at a dead-end street. We need time to spiritually reconstruct our society. But we don't have the time anymore. The processes have been started, the buttons have been pushed and thus function independently now. The people, the politicians have become slaves of the systems they have erected themselves. The computer has already taken the lead over Man. In order for the computer to cease functioning, it would take spiritual work for which we don't have the time anymore. The only hope is that, in the last moment when there is still time to turn off the computer, Man will be enlightened from above. Only that could save us.

Q: *We constantly fight something and protect ourselves from something, because the dead-end street has become very narrow. The walls are closing in on us. Our conversation is a perfect example. You are fighting me and I am fighting you.*
T: To be honest with you, I didn't think you would come. But now you are here and we have to speak to each other. Yes, Man is fighting the wrong enemy. The woman fights the man, the man fights the woman, the man fights other men, the woman fights other women. One country is fighting another, one group is fighting against the development of missiles, another group fights something else, and so we all fight something, instead of fighting the fight with ourselves. We are our worst enemy. This is where the fight has to take place. I am also my most terrifying enemy and I keep asking myself if I will besiege myself or not. This is the meaning of my life. I will not be able to calm down before I know if I have besieged myself. I was born to besiege myself or else be besieged.

Q: *I am especially interested in your new film* Nostalghia. *Were you concerned with the problem of emigration?*
T: It is not an emigration film, it is a film about nostalgia, about the feeling one calls homesickness, the longing for the homeland. That is all. This is what the film is about.

Q: *What does "homeland" mean to you?*
T: Home is the country in which one was born, where one grew up, with whose culture one is connected, where one is rooted. I spent time in the USA and that country astonished me–a land without roots. Rootlessness is so visible there! On one hand it makes the country dynamic, free of prejudices. On the other hand, spirituality is missing. People start a new life somewhere else and break the bonds with the past. This is a deep issue. In America I found reassurance for the thoughts I am concerned with in *Nostalghia*. It is unbelievably hard to live like that. All the problems begin with stepping out of the historical context. This is what the movie is about. How can someone live normally, fully, if he breaks with his roots? In Russian, "nostalghia" is an illness, a life-threatening disease.

Q: *It is very tempting to break with everything.*
T: Tempting? That it is.

Q: *It is also an opportunity.*
T: It is not an opportunity.

Q: *It isn't?*
T: It isn't. Irena, there are no opportunities there.

Q: *An opportunity for individualism?*
T: Man is not ready for it yet.

Q: *Our century is a nomadic one. The blending of peoples is happening more and more; there are more and more emigrants. Maybe we'll overcome the nostalgia in a few centuries.*
T: One by one that will naturally happen. But the problem lies deeper. And I am sure you will not disagree when I say that it is abnormal that

the planet is divided into spheres of influence. This is abnormal because it was not Man who created this world. Man has no rights to it. His right is only to live on this earth and grow spiritually, and not to divide the planet with barbed wire and maintain the division with nuclear weapons. This activity is inhuman. And this circumstance has produced other problems: nostalgia, civilization, confrontation. What else could have come from this position? If I believe that I am right and my neighbor is wrong, if I completely disagree with him and am unwilling to reason with him, it will end in an open confrontation. There is no other possibility. We live in an inhuman manner. The film *Nostalghia* is concerned with the question: How should we live? How could we find ways to come to an agreement in this divided world? It can only be achieved through mutual sacrifice. Someone who is not able to sacrifice can't expect anything.

Q: *Are you yourself able to sacrifice?*
T: That's hard to say. I am just as unable as anyone else. But I hope I will be able to do so. I hope so, because if I die without having proved this ability to myself, it will be sad.

Q: *And how will you achieve that?*
T: How? I don't know. By living in a decent manner in my striving for what I believe in. But my profession is a hindrance. I am not sure that what I do professionally is really necessary, if I should go on doing it.

Q: *What would you like to do?*
T: Sometimes my field of work seems ridiculous to me. There are things that are more important. How to approach those things, how to find yourself in them, if there is a positive way in art at all, that is the question. So one educates others without being ready oneself, that bothers me. Leo Tolstoy was troubled by this question all his life.

Q: *How do your films reflect your personal developments?*
T: I believe I am reflected in my films, that is unquestionable. If there is a development, I don't know. I could simply not produce films without bringing in my personality.

Q: *When I compare your films, I get the impression that you are working towards an ascetic style.*

T: Yes, that is correct. I would like to be like that. In my latest film I think everything is expressed more simply than in my earlier work. To you, the viewer, one can never do it right. However it is, there will always be millions of questions. I don't know anymore.

Q: *Do you think of the viewer at all?*

T: I have never thought of the viewer. How could I? What should I think? Should I educate him? Or will I find out what one John Smith in London or a certain Vassil Ivanov in Moscow thinks? I would be the biggest phony to pretend that I know what someone else thinks, what his world is. If I want to do anything at all, I can only do it my way and take the viewer as my equal. So I don't compromise. If I am uncertain about something, I believe that the viewer feels the same way and I try to clarify it in a film for myself and for the viewer. I am neither smarter nor stupider than the viewer. My dignity can be harmed as well as the viewer's. Of course, one can make films with the consideration of the purse. Nothing is easier. But that is not my profession. I will never concern myself with that.

Q: *What does it feel like to be in a foreign country, to work creatively with people?*

T: I made my film *Nostalghia* in a foreign country. Basically I don't see any difference. There is a difference but it is not significant.

Q: *The Czech director Milos Forman has worked as an immigrant in the USA since 1968. He says that the artist in the Eastern Bloc is under ideological pressure and in the West he is under commercial pressure. What do you think about this?*

T: Yes, I feel great commercial pressure here. But I am not able to make films under outside pressure.

Q: *You really manage to work without compromise?*

T: I don't think I can deal with compromises, to be concerned with them in my work. So it doesn't make any difference to me where I work. I know I am not able to fulfill orders. If I am not dealing with my own ideas, I won't be able to realize them. Of course there are great hindrances.

Q: *Your father, Arseni Tarkovsky, is a famous contemporary lyric poet. His sphere, the sphere of poetics, is eternal. Your sphere of film is subjugated by the changes of time. How does it feel to be so close with one and the same name?*
T: That doesn't bother me at all. I disagree with you—in art there is no distinction between a more or less important field. Only quality counts. There are good and bad verses, and good and bad films.

Q: *It seems to me that you work with symbols. In* Solaris, *the hero returns to his parents' house and it rains. The rain is strong, it penetrates the house, it drips on the father. Does that rain signify home, does it mean past memories?*
T: Symbolism is a difficult subject. I am an enemy of symbolism. Symbolism is too narrow a notion to me, because symbols are there to be decoded. But an artistic image cannot be decoded. It is an equivalent of the world we live in. The rain in *Solaris* is not a symbol, it is just rain that grows in significance for the hero at a certain point. It doesn't symbolize anything. It expresses something. That rain is an artistic image. The notion of the symbol is too confusing for me.

Q: *What are your plans for the future? Will you stay in the West for the time being?*
T: Yes, but I don't know yet where I will make my new film. I will make a film version of *Hamlet.* The money is being raised by a Swedish film institute . . . the same one that also finances Bergman.

Q: *Does this mean that you might go to Sweden?*
T: Not necessarily. My dream is to make a film about *Hamlet.*

Q: *Do you already know how?*
T: Basically, yes, but I don't want to talk about it. It is too early. In the first place, I want to do *Hamlet*, and then maybe another film. I have yet to write the scenario for *Hamlet.* To do that I would like to stay in the West for about three years.

Q: *Without returning to the Soviet Union?*
T: I want to return with *Hamlet* in my hands.

Q: *Should the film be in English?*
T: I think it should be in English.

Q: *Are you thinking of specific actors?*
T: No, I haven't thought about actors yet.

Q: *And why do you want to make a film on* Hamlet?
T: Because *Hamlet* deals with the contemporary problem: the most significant question, the answer of which will determine if humanity will survive or commit suicide. Of course, I have to find an equivalent to Shakespeare in my own genre. I have to find my own form to deal with the subject, a different dramaturgy.

The Twentieth Century and the Artist

V. ISHIMOV AND R. SHEJKO/1984

In 1984 under the auspices of the St. James Festival, a retrospective of Andrei Tarkovsky's films was arranged. In one of the London churches Tarkovsky delivered the speech "The Word of the Apocalypse." Here he met with viewers, spoke on the topic of "The Creation of a Film and the Artist's Responsibility," and then answered questions. Today we draw our readers' attention to a record of two such meetings.

The First Meeting

TARKOVSKY: Today there will be no film, for today I will simply chat with you. And I will begin—before you ask any questions—with how I can barely conceive what would become of us artists if we were completely free. This would be something akin to deepwater fish suddenly being dragged up to the surface. Some years ago, I made a film about Roublev, who was a brilliant artist. Now, in our time, it is absolutely impossible to fathom how he worked within the harshest limits of religious canons, which subsequently forced him to paint as it was decreed in the so-called illuminated originals. Thus a specific stamp existed for every icon, and it was simply impossible to violate this in the formal sense of composition and color. It is inconceivable that despite all this he turned out to be a genius, especially in comparison to his predecessors. In general, freedom is an awfully strange thing.

From *Iskusstvo Kino*, no. 4 (1989): 88–106. Translated from Russian by Tim Harte.

For a whole year I had to work in Italy, where freedom means that people get shot; those who do the shooting are sent to jail, but they walk away very quickly, since there are millions of ways to defend such criminals and only one way to punish them. But I am not for draconian measures, for I only want to say that in order to be free, it is simply necessary to be so. You do not have to ask anyone's permission. This is very simple. But, nevertheless, we really don't know how to be free. For the freest people are those who demand nothing from life. They demand a good deal from themselves. They put enormous pressure on themselves, but not on those around them. I don't want you to get the wrong impression of what I'm saying, I'm talking about inner freedom in the moral sense of the word. I do not intend to polemicize with traditional English democracy or the anarchy that exists there, but in any case I'm talking about that freedom, which throughout history has been entrusted to people who have sacrificed themselves to the period and society in which they live.

I am dwelling on this topic because, as I already noted, of having made my last picture. I have always wanted to recognize those who are internally free, irrespective of the fact that they have been surrounded by people lacking this freedom. It is often said that one has to be strong, but does anyone really understand what it means to be strong? I have always wanted to witness a strong person portrayed as weak in the generally accepted meaning of this word. Thus in *Stalker* I decided to show through the protagonist just such an individual. He is very weak, but he has one quality that makes him invincible, namely faith. He is convinced that he must serve people. And thus he becomes invincible. To speak broadly about the fact that a person can perish and simultaneously lose everything is a position, as you probably understand, that is untenable. From my point of view, we seize upon our profession not so much to convince ourselves in the truth of our ability to say what we want, but rather to demonstrate our will to serve. I am simply amazed by artists who insist that they have created themselves. This is simply not true, for time creates us, as do the people amidst whom we live. And if we succeed with something, that is only because others are in need of what we have produced. And the more success we have with something, the more people require that we express it. So it goes without saying, as a result of this we in principle never win out, others win. We always lose.

Well, I wanted to say these few words before you begin to ask your questions. I would like for our meeting to be more of a conversation than simply you listening to some speech, especially since I don't really know how to deliver a speech.

I cannot imagine my life as so free that I can do whatever I want. I need to do things that seem to me to be most important and most necessary, at least to the extent to which I define this necessity. The only way to communicate with you and with all viewers is to remain myself. It is absolutely impossible to communicate on any other level. Of course, in cinema this is very difficult, since 75 to 80 percent of all viewers believe that we should entertain them. True, it is not clear why they do. But nevertheless, this is a fact, and on this fact depends the amount of money they will give us for our future productions. We find ourselves caught in a divide: on the one hand, we should be ourselves, but on the other hand, even at a minimum we ought to justify the expenditures of the producer and the distributor, so that someone will want to do business with us in the future. You have to admit that the situation is fairly bleak. We have stopped respecting this 75 percent of all viewers to such an extent that we are immediately prepared to entertain them. But we need to bear with this 75 percent a bit more and convince them that no one needs to entertain them. They will get used to this very quickly. (laughter) Unfortunately, though, not every director thinks the way I do. Well, imagine for a second that we all agreed among ourselves and stopped entertaining the public. And if we were not to die out, we would prevail. We would succeed in transforming this 75 percent.

I understand that you who are in the audience today, with the exception of perhaps a few of you, are those, I sense (laughter), who belong to the 25 percent. It is easy to communicate with you. But it turns out to be such a horrid experience when I meet with audiences who look for entertainment in cinema. I've had to attend such gatherings. Afterwards, I was ill for a long time to come. (laughter) But today I have a cheerful gathering, for sitting here is an outstanding English director—I have long respected this artist [Lindsay Anderson], not to mention respect for my distributor. But I should note that I look very, very optimistically on the distribution of my films, because I have always presented a measure of resistance, leaving viewers without entertainment. I feel that if people go to watch my films they already have a good idea of what they're going to see.

In any case, thank you for coming here, and now I await your questions. For they will most likely give me reason to speak in a far more interesting fashion than I did just now. (*laughter*)

Q: *What is cinema's aim, if not entertainment?*
T: I will be brief. As they say, brevity is the sister of talent. Isn't cinema an art?

Q: *Yes.*
T: Art has never had entertainment as its aim. In several cases, paradoxical ones we might say, Matisse pronounced that he was like some sort of cushy sofa. But it seems to me that he was fooling around and wanted to fool those intending to buy his paintings. If cinema is an art, then, as with all art, it has completely different aims. But which specific aims? To express and explain to oneself and simultaneously to everyone else around what a person lives for. What is the point of life. To explain life and the reason for one's appearance on this planet . . . What ominous silence . . . (*laughter*)

Q: *To what extent was* The Mirror *an experiment in montage?*
T: You know, I never had the goal of conducting an experiment. Cinema is not a science, and we cannot permit ourselves to conduct experiments that do not always bring about successful results. No one will give us money for such experiments. In any case, in art no experiments exist. . . . Method will never become the aim of art. Regardless of the fact that in the twentieth century artists are occupied namely with this emphasis on method and an obsessive, completely unbridled exhibitionism. Very unusual exhibitionism. Paul Valéry, the French critic, poet, and essayist wrote about this very nicely. He said that in our time the stroke and style have become the content of easel work. I think his work is called "Degas's Guest." And he's right. Well, let's recall Picasso. He would do a drawing, sign his name, sell the work for a good deal of money, and then give this money to France's Communist Party. Amazing! But it seems to me that this has nothing to do with art.

I don't know what happened, why art lost its mystery in the twentieth century. Why it was that the artist suddenly wanted to obtain everything. The artist has written his first quatrain and he already wants it
published. Earlier, like Kafka, the artist would write his novels and die,
leaving a will instructing his friend and executor to destroy all his works.
Fortunately, the friend destroys the will. You might say that Kafka also
belongs to the twentieth century. Yes, this is the twentieth century, but
he does not belong to it. Ethically, he belongs to the previous century.
That's why he suffered so much. He was a man who was not prepared
for his time. So my main point is that a true artist does not experiment
or search—he finds. Because if he does not find, his work is completely
in vain. When you talk about montage in regard to experimentation, I
ought to answer that in the case of *The Mirror*, there was never a problem
with montage. Or rather, there was no experimentation.

To be quite honest, when I shot the picture and had a mountain of
material, I edited things, made one version, a second one, a tenth one, a
twentieth, and it turned out that the film did not exist. There was no
problem here with montage experimentation. The picture was simply not
working out. It was not working out, I would even say, in a terribly catastrophic sense of the word. It was obvious that the material possessed certain qualities that I couldn't control. Editing the picture I thought about
dramatic composition. Only having made twenty edited versions did I
realize that I had to try and paste together my material according to a
completely different principle, without any regard for logic. This was the
twenty-first version. And this is the version that you have seen on the
movie screen. Once I had seen the picture, I immediately understood that
this time I had avoided tragic failure. How this all transpired, I don't
know. But I assure you that I at first had the impression that all the material had been shot improperly. And when I speak of versions, I am talking
about versions in which episodes, rather than individual shots, were
switched. I was not even thinking about the details of individual shots.
So there you have the history of the film's editing.

Q: *Is your last film, which was made in Italy, a Soviet-Italian
co-production?*
T: The film is Italian, shot with money from Italian radio and television. But I did produce it and Oleg Yankovsky appeared in the main

role (by the way, you can see him right here in London at this festival in the two films, *Nostalghia* and in *Flights in Dreams and in Reality*). Moreover, my wife Larissa Pavlona, who has made all of my films with me, worked as my assistant. All of this is sufficient grounds for calling the film a co-production.

Q: *Jointly with "Sovinfilm" [Soviet Information Film]? What does that mean?*
T: "Sovinfilm" is the organization that mandates all foreign connections for our film industry.

Q: *Did you feel freer in Italy than in the Soviet Union in terms of being able to shoot the film according to your own style? Did you feel any commercial pressure?*
T: And did you see *Nostalghia*? I assume you saw it. In terms of the work, I do not sense a big difference. All film people are extremely similar to one another. I have often been completely amazed that even the types and personalities of people working together on a film manage to be the same. The profession leaves its imprint. But I would not say that it was really so easy to make a film in Italy. This does not mean that I found it more difficult to work in Italy than in the Soviet Union. I have somehow gotten used to the fact that the director's profession is simply that of a waiter who is expected to carry in a mountain of plates and not break them. If you have some sort of project, it is insanely difficult to see it through to completion, for after your initial meetings with the film crew you completely forget about your initial project. Therefore your task is to not forget that which you intended to do, no matter what happens. In the film world everything is done so that after the first week you have completely lost the ability to understand where you are and what you are doing. Although I should mention that in the Soviet Union I never had to think about money, but here in Italy, forgive me, I have had to think about it endlessly. I have heard the word "money" far more often than "hello" or "goodbye." (*laughter*) This is difficult. If you learn how to turn off your consciousness when they talk to you about money, then everything falls into place. You simply have to become an idiot when money is mentioned. In any case, forgive me, I'll finish this thought, be it difficult or not so difficult . . . In cinema it

is so hard to work that it makes no difference whether things become a bit easier or a bit harder. At one time before the war, I think it was the Americans who made up a questionnaire on what people thought were the most destructive, most dangerous professions. In first place were test pilots, and in second place, film directors.

Q: *You have complained that 80 percent of all viewers see cinema as enter-tainment. At the same time you have said that cinema has been summoned to explain the meaning of life. A paradox exists in the fact that for a large group of people your explication of the creation of your films is so complicated that they find it all completely incomprehensible. But you nevertheless want to explain these global problems to the world.*

T: I don't think I'm the only one faced with this situation. I don't think of myself as so different from my colleagues. This is the first thing. Secondly, I am personally satisfied that I have that 25 to 35 percent of all viewers. For me this is perfectly fine. You probably know that in Moscow we have two large, quite famous concert halls. One is the Large Hall of the Moscow Conservatory and the second is Tchaikovsky Hall. Approximately nine to ten million people live in Moscow. People can hear Bach, Mozart, and Beethoven. And somehow these two halls suf-fice in satisfying the spiritual needs of these ten million Muscovites. Regardless of the fact that masterpieces are played and the composers are so renowned, no one is beating down the doors and the audience does not even increase to a million. Similarly, there is no need to pub-lish Pushkin or Shakespeare in gigantic editions. We all say that we can't live without them, but to tell you the truth, does more than 20 to 30 percent of the population really read Pushkin and Shakespeare? I mean, that is, do they reread them? As workers in the cinema we find ourselves in a far worse situation. Look at what is occurring today. For many years film directors did what the public expected from them. And it ended up that the public no longer wanted to watch this work. But the situation is even worse now, because if we were to suddenly show works we *want* to show to an already disappointed public, they will have no desire to watch these either. For they themselves have changed so much, they have already been corrupted. In order for them to become like they once were, say, fifteen years ago, we must waste another twenty years. And thus, the film industry's dependence on viewers can lead to complete uncertainty in terms of what films one has to shoot to justify production expenses. But at the same time I am assured of my 25 to 30 percent of all viewers.

Q: *In* The Mirror *and* Stalker *one senses the theme of freedom and a feeling of unsteadiness in the surroundings. What connection is there with the inner freedom, of which you spoke, and the correlation with weakness, which you have contrasted with force?*
T: When I say "weakness," I have in mind first and foremost the absence of aggression. This is really the ability to sacrifice oneself. Because in the end . . .

Q: *Do you have in mind weakness or the acceptance of something?*
T: Acceptance, yes, yes.

Q: *Weakness is probably not the most appropriate word. For aggression is its opposite. Acceptance would probably be more accurate.*
T: I agree. But this is a problem of translation, and not my problem. I did understand you. But the fact of the matter is that in principle humans have grasped that they first and foremost want to demand something from others, to teach others how to express their desires. Just as I am interested in people who direct all of this toward themselves. Only from that moment on, from that point on, can humankind call any movement optimistic. Everything else can only lead us to catastrophe. This is what I wanted to say in all the films about which I have spoken. Humans are the center of the world, the center of the universe. Yet not in the sense that your consider yourself more important than someone else, but in fact the opposite.

Q: *Would you be able to say something about your plans and your future film projects?*
T: There are plans, naturally. And there are many of them. But not to bore you, then, I hope for instance to stage *Hamlet* in English.

LINDSAY ANDERSON: *Great! Why not?*
T: "Why not?" Mr. Anderson said. That's wonderful!

Q: *Your Soviet films have stood out with the tangible presence of scope and space. In them you have conveyed a fear of this space. Isn't this right?*

T: Space—in what sense? In a literal sense? My God, it simply scares me. Until now I haven't even been able to release myself of the spaces that I was forced to overcome when I made *Roublev*. If you didn't see it, then that explains everything. If you saw it, then your question is not a good one. *(laughter)* In terms of my most recent films and the claustrophobia about which you speak, Hamlet said it best in his time: "Imprison me in a nutshell, and I will become the sovereign of infinite space." I have translated this into Russian, for it would be difficult to remember Shakespeare's actual words. But you don't need to recall the line. Rather, you should read Shakespeare.

Q: *How did you come upon the idea to make a film about Roublev?*

T: I always have difficulty answering questions about why I made this or that film. Because the problem of *what and why* has never been a real problem for me. It is probably because of this that I don't remember what served as the impetus to produce this or another picture. There was never any specific moment that determined my plans in favor of Roublev. I just don't recall how it happened. It somehow happened without a clamor.

Q: *When you spoke at the National Cinema, you stated that the profession of the filmmaker is similar to that of a poet. Analogous to the role of the poet. Could you explain?*

T: Of course I can. As a matter of fact, Blok, a well-known poet at the end of the nineteenth century and beginning of the twentieth century, although he belongs more to the twentieth, stated that the poet's mission is to create harmony out of chaos. To create harmonious works out of the world's chaos. Pushkin also wrote about this in "Mozart and Salieri." Cinema in its essence, in its pictorial composition, is primarily a poetic art. For it is able to make do without maintaining any literal meaning, without normal sequential logic. Even without what we call dramatic composition. Cinema's specificity consists in the fact that the medium has been called upon to fix and record time. Time in a philosophical, poetic, and literal sense. Cinema came into being at the end of the last century and beginning of the twentieth century. It emerged at precisely the same time that humans began to sense a deficit of time. We have already grown accustomed to living in a terribly compressed world. It seems to me that a person, let's say, from the nineteenth or eighteenth century could not exist in our epoch. He would simply die from the pressure that time would place on him. That is, he would be forced to function much more quickly in a physical and moral sense. And cinema in its essence has been called upon to give poetic meaning to this problem. So look, cinema is the only art that literally imprints time. In other words, it is theoretically possible to look over the same filmstrip an infinite number of times. Thus it is like a matrix of time. And in this sense, just as the problem of rhythm plays an enormous role in poetry, the problem of length and tempo in cinema takes on its own special meaning. It is in this sense that time expresses itself. This is an incredibly interesting problem. In a certain sense each art is poetic in its highest and finest forms. Leonardo is a poet in the figurative arts, a poetic genius. For it would be ridiculous to call Leonardo an artist, ridiculous to call Bach a composer, ridiculous to call Shakespeare a playwright, and ridiculous to call Tolstoy a writer. They are poets. There is a difference. And I have this in mind when I talk about how cinema has its own poetic essence. For there is part of life, part of the universe, which we would never know or comprehend through other forms and genres of art. For cinema can do that which music and all the other forms and genres of art cannot do. And vice versa. Therefore it is impossible to say that art grows old. True art does not grow old. And I, as a professional director, strive to interpret poetically aesthetic and moral issues that seize my attention.

Q: *When you prepare for your films, do you plan and record all shots and scenes or do they arise in the process of shooting the film?*
T: I seem to work in two stages. I initially develop my prospective filming plan, but when I come to the filming site, it turns out that life is much richer than my imagination and that I need to change everything. But now I am already beginning to understand that if you go to the film location unprepared, you become freer. In the past I did preliminary work because I did not have a sufficiently professional conception of my own creativity. Today I fear that this conception has become too rigid for me. And it makes sense to simply stop thinking about this.

Q: *At an international film school seminar you stated that women do not have enough spirituality to be filmmakers.*
T: You know, if I said this, that women do not have sufficient spirit to create, then today I ought to say that women *do* have sufficient spirit to *not* create. The trouble is that men do not have sufficient spirit to not occupy ourselves with creating things. This is how we differ from women. In other words, a woman wants to create out of a surplus of spirit, while a man creates out of a need for self-affirmation, due to the fact that he lacks spirituality. Just as I differ from you! But at the same time, if I were asked about my attitude toward female directors, I would not respond, for you simply need to turn your attention to the history of art.

Q: *What does Mrs. Tarkovsky have to say about this matter?*
T: My wife doesn't even understand what we're talking about. She obviously shares my point of view. No, in any case I want to state that everything and anything is possible. But one gets very few chances.

Q: *Why did you decide to stage an opera after you had worked in cinema?*
T: Namely because I had not done an opera up to that point.

Q: *What qualities are you looking for in an actor? What is your attitude toward actors?*
T: What is my approach to actors? Or how do I choose them?

Q: *What is your working approach toward actors?*
T: I am prepared to give the actor complete freedom if the actor demonstrates complete subordination to the concept before beginning work. The fact that we find ourselves on different sides of the concept suggests the impossibility of what they so often note: be it some sort of dictatorial behavior on the part of the director or, on the other hand, complete non-interference in actor issues. . . . In short, I am intolerant as a director if the actor does not share my point of view on an idea, on the conception of a future film. And I adore and love those actors who share my views, and I give them complete freedom. Among all my actors and all those with whom I have worked, I have only come into conflict with two.

Q: *I am amazed by the interest of Russians and Soviets in* Hamlet.
T: If you are amazed by Russians' interest in *Hamlet*, then I am amazed by the absence of interest in *Hamlet* among the English.

Q: *Is it specifically* Hamlet, *in contrast to Shakespeare's other works, that attracts Russians?*
T: *Hamlet* is the finest dramatic and poetic work of art existing in the world.

Q: *Why is it the best and why is it such an attractive work?*
T: Because in this drama we are presented with the most important problem existing during Shakespeare's time and up to that time, as well as forever since. This problem revolves around the fact that Shakespeare's drama does not yield to any production, that is, no matter who stages *Hamlet*, one always experiences defeat. Yet I too want to stage *Hamlet*. But it is impossible to do anything. This is a huge secret. For instance, I believe that the significance of *Hamlet* hinges on how a highly spiritual man has to live among people who subsist at a much lower level. A man of the future is forced to live in the past. In the true past. And the drama of Hamlet does not revolve around the fact that he is doomed to die and thus perishes, but rather that tragically the protagonist is threatened by a moral, spiritual death. And because of this, he is impelled to reject his spiritual pretensions and become an ordinary murderer. He has to stop living, and in other words, to commit suicide. That is, to not carry out his moral duty.

Q: *What are your favorite films?*
T: I really love Bresson, Bergman, Antonioni, Mizoguchi, Vigo, Buñuel, and whom else? But I'm not telling you anything new. There are five, six, or seven directors . . .

Q: *We see few Soviet films here. Yet how often do they show foreign films in the Soviet Union, and which foreign films?*
T: I am afraid that we see few foreign films, fewer than you see, and they are not always of a high quality. It is difficult for me to explain why this is so, but I fear that good films are expensive.

Q: *Which classic Soviet directors do you like?*

T: Well, I worship what Alexander Dovzhenko did in the silent era, and among the first sound films, I really love the early pictures of Kalatozov. His *Salt for Svanetia* is an amazing film. From the classic works, I have named just about everything. I don't really like Eisenstein, for it seems to me that he is calculating and awfully cerebral . . .

Q: *Wasn't he an experimenter?*

T: I don't know. But I really love the Soviet directors Sergei Paradjanov and Otar Iosseliani.

Q: *What is the main idea of your film* Solaris? *You claim that you always have a precise idea, but in this film I myself sensed only beauty and mystery.* Solaris *has been compared to other science-fiction films. It seems to me that the music in* Solaris *runs counter to the film.*

T: If I tell you what the film's central idea was, I am sure that it will not run counter to your impression. Because, unlike the main idea of Lem's novel, the idea in our film was the following: human beings have to remain human beings, even if they find themselves in inhumane conditions.

Q: *Did you use the choral prelude to Bach's "I Beseech You, O God" because it was important for the film* Solaris? *It seems to me that this is paradoxical in terms of the film's central idea.*

T: What could be more natural than to express this idea of humanity with the help of Bach's music? I do not understand why this runs counter to the main idea of the film.

Q: *Was there a religious, Christian agenda in your choice of music?*

T: Every art carries within it a religious purpose.

Q: *Why do you believe art has a religious purpose?*

T: Because it does not conceive logically, nor does it formulate the logic of behavior, but it does seem to express the postulate of faith. It postulates faith. In other words, one has to receive an artistic image on faith, in contrast to any logical discourse. And what is more, if Tolstoy, let's say, took some sort of conception or idea as the basis for his work, given his work and its form he would ruin his artistic schema. And what is more, we do not always understand or agree with an artistic idea, but the artwork nevertheless exists. It is as if the work overcomes its underlying idea, an idea that seems insignificant in comparison to the image of the world established in the work and perceived by us as a revelation. In other words, art exists despite any logical conception. Look, we often say that a certain artist, writer, musician, or director is a philosopher. But this is only a word. An artist, in fact, is not really a philosopher. And if we analyze his philosophical ideas, then it turns out that, in the first place, he is not original, and secondly, he obviously uses various well-known ideas or at least draws upon them. For he is really not a philosopher, but rather a poet. What constitutes a poet? This is a person who has the psychology and imagination of a child. Of course one can say, looking at a child, that he or she is a philosopher, but only in some sort of completely conditional sense of the word. So far as the artist and the work of art reveal the world and force us either to accept and believe in it or else reject it, then the only thing we can speak about is the religious impression a true work of art makes on a person. For it affects the soul of a person and a person's spiritual foundation.

Q: *You also said earlier that art is interested in the meaning of life and is aimed at elucidating the world, yet I do not sense this elucidation in your films. There is depth and mystery in them. The public acknowledges this mystery most of all. Isn't the process of perception religious due to the fact that we do not know the answer, for* Solaris *does not provide an answer?*
T: If a sense of mystery arises for you then that for me is an enormous compliment. In my mind, if the viewer carries away the idea that life is a mystery then I am happy. Because for a huge number of people, life today does not represent any sort of mystery.

Q: *The paradox, then, is that elucidation is mystery.*
T: No, if you see for yourself some aspect of my mystery, watching the film, this means that I succeeded in expressing my approach to life. For there is no deeper, more mysterious, and more critical mystery than the mystery of our existence. And if everyone . . . or many, will think in this fashion, then life will change.

Q: *Is this the crux of your film?*
T: No, this is really a supplementary intonation.

Q: *What is your opinion of opera?*
T: My opinion is a very strange one. I don't know a more unnatural genre than opera. And because of this I would like to spend some time in the skin of a person who roils about in the cauldron of opera, so I could understand what it's all about. So I could try to find some sort of logic, something real. What could be stranger than someone expressing human emotion by singing like a bird?

Q: *That often occurs in real life.*
T: No, I assure you, that rarely happens.

Q: *Now you're speaking in terms of realism.*
T: I'm speaking in terms of life's truth.

Q: *Is this an argument or a question?*
T: In terms of conventions on the whole, then of course one can sing. But something is not right in this genre. Something is not as it should be. It's not a coincidence that people say that they went to the opera to listen to Verdi. For if you announced that you went to watch the opera, they would say that you're simply a poorly educated, unintelligent person. Well, simply stated, upon entering the opera hall you need to close your eyes and listen to the music. And many do just that. I have heard from many people that once they open their eyes they are simply frightened by what is transpiring on stage. In fact for everyone this is terribly unnatural. But as I said, I would like to spend time in the skin of people who feel at home in this art. It is true, however, that I did not choose the best opera to begin down this path. I chose *Boris Godunov* by Mussorgsky and Pushkin. Why not something better? For this is a very dramatic opera. If I suddenly decided to stage, let's say, Wagner or, on the other hand, an Italian opera, it would be easier for me to demonstrate what I have in mind when I speak about my opinion of opera. But because I took on *Boris Godunov*, I again have to develop various dramatic, psychological, and moral categories, along with musical categories of course. And this, as one might say, makes my experiment at

this moment very difficult. It's as if I have rejected opera in a psycho-logical and dramatic sense and, at the same time, I must do everything I can to develop these two specific qualities in my production. In short, I got caught. I fell into a trap.

(*Ovation*)

The Second Meeting

TARKOVSKY: It somehow happened that the topic of our conversation, the question of an artist's responsibility, had been established sometime earlier. But while I was traveling here from Italy, I realized that this is not so feasible. What does the responsibility of an artist mean? Everything depends on how extensively artists sense this responsibility within themselves. How can one demand this of others! Even the small-est demand would be indiscreet. Therefore I think that it makes sense to talk about something related, yet a bit different: the role of art in contemporary life.

Of course, it's very clear that in our time art finds itself in a state of deep depression. This is not something that depends upon various social conditions and circumstances, or on the public's lack of interest. The roots of this problem lie elsewhere. For the public is interested in art, and artists search for the path and possibility of communicating with the public, yet both public and artist suffer from insufficient con-tact and insufficient potential for interaction. Those who are closely connected with art understand these problems. Apparently, the prob-lem is that art is becoming less and less spiritual. It has already set its sights on something completely different, and this is not something it needs to seek out or strive for. And to a large degree, this hinges on the public, which in the end influences that which transpires in art.

Owing to a prevailing sense of conformity, we have gotten to the point where art is treated as entertainment. Naturally, when we look at drama and its history, it's clear that the theater, to varying degrees, has always served this aim. (I'm not talking about ancient or medieval mys-tery plays.) Cinema from the outset was in principle a commercial art. But strange developments are occurring in cinema. I would even say cat-astrophic developments. For viewers have gotten what they wanted, and, in general, they have stopped going to the cinema. And it is fortunate

that they have stopped going. For in this there is a certain critique of
the circumstances: viewers are no longer satisfied with what today is
classified as contemporary cinema. And in the other arts, for instance
the figurative arts, the situation is also very, very disheartening. In
short, this crisis has arisen out of our lack of spirituality.

Everyone knows that it is impossible to make a living with non-
commercial art, that is, art focused on the inner world of human beings.
Famous writers are now forced to write screenplays in order to make
a commercial picture; those who ten years ago achieved well-known
successes now produce work of wretched quality. In other words, there's
no need to speak of any sort of renaissance.

This, perhaps, is the most significant problem tormenting me. What
can I do? Am I guilty of this and to what extent?

I am guilty, as are many of my colleagues, in that we forget what aim
art should serve, thus jeopardizing our creative careers. Recently I had
the opportunity to meet with a group of young people at the Centro
Sperimentale di Cinematografia in Rome and I was amazed by the following. One young man, who plans to be an artist and a filmmaker,
admitted that he had enrolled in film school knowing beforehand that
he would be a prostitute. And this is essentially the same for everyone,
almost without exception.

A celebrated social motif of nineteenth century literature is the story
of the young man who sets out to make his fortune in the big city. This
classical theme is well known in American and French literature, and
every other literature. The story concludes in a more or less dramatic
fashion, as the hero loses his illusion; many novels deal with this spiritual drama. Today young people just beginning their lives in art and
working as students know how to conduct themselves to further their
careers in the field of commercial cinema. This is how the thoughts of
young people intending to become filmmakers have changed in our
time. This has occurred for various reasons.

All of you know that, unlike the East—by this I mean the Far East
with its deep, traditional, Hindu and Japanese cultures—the West has
always been very pragmatic. In the end, democratic gains in the West,
which gave humans the possibility to experience freedom, essentially
deprived Westerners of having faith in anyone except themselves. In a
certain sense, this Western democracy is egotistical. This, in general, is

also the case with Western culture. It is a well-known feature, and I do not want to dwell on it too long.

What can we say constitutes a masterpiece in the West? Even during the Renaissance. It is always the cry of the human soul, which expresses a thousand desires: look how happy I am, look how unhappy I am, look how I suffer, how I love, look what villains encircle me, look how I struggle against evil, look how I perish under the weight of evil, look how I prevail. In other words—me, me, me, me, me . . . (If I say something wrong, you will have the opportunity to ask me questions and take exception to what I say.)

When we talk of classical Eastern art, we're not talking about a set hundred years of its history, we're talking about two or three thousand years. Take, for instance, Eastern music . . . In my last picture *Nostalghia*, which I made in Italy, I came across Daoist music from approximately sixth century BC. I put it into my film. This is amazing music, not to mention its inherent formal qualities. There in the East, inversely, all meaning centers on disappearing and blending in. There is a certain introversion of Eastern spirituality expressed in this music. A certain spiritual collapse, when the personal draws the entire surrounding world into itself. Thus the entire world breathes, but again in a spiritual sense.

I want to designate, quite boldly and crudely, this watershed between Western and Eastern cultures in order to emphasize how this difference looks today. None of you will take exception to the idea that all of world civilization rests on the Eastern culture of China, Japan, and India. And that Eastern barbarism runs counter to the West's love of freedom and democracy. I do, however, agree with those perceptive listeners today who note that I'm not entirely right since in Western music we have figures like Bach. But, you know, Bach is a "black sheep." He has nothing in common with tradition, and, on the contrary, he breaks with traditions in a spiritual sense. His relationship with God is absolutely outside of civilization. And it might be that this exception only underscores my idea that in the West it's impossible to lose oneself in one's creativity, to sacrifice oneself. For this is the proper action of a real artist. Take for example Russia's icons from the thirteenth, fourteenth, and fifteenth centuries. There is not one icon that has been signed by the artist. The icon painter did not consider himself an artist. If he was able to paint icons, he thanked God, for he believed that with his handi-craft and his professional trade he served God. He would essentially pray, and this was the essence of his work. In other words, I'm speaking about the lack of ego in the creative process.

You know, the entire Renaissance, let's take for instance the Italian Renaissance, represents unbelievably inflated ambition. Not that I'm belittling the achievements of the Western Renaissance. I simply want to say that the interdependence in which Eastern and Western classical art was once situated is the same interdependence and the same gap found today between contemporary Western art and classical Western art. Movement from East to West continually occurs, but from the West comes nothing. In short, loss, dissipation, and spiritual entropy are all occurring. I do all I can to welcome and embrace Western democracy, but I must tell you that it has deprived humans of experiencing their spirituality. In the existentialism of the Western intellectual, spirituality is not obligatory. Forgive me, I am not criticizing, for I could criticize other aspects of our life much more, aspects that I know very well, but I'm not talking about these things. Since we find ourselves in the West today, I would like to talk about that which is most crucial for you and me right now.

The freedom and guarantees given to human beings through Western democracy have somehow made them very, very spiritually weak. But please don't think that I adhere to the point of view that in order to achieve a high level of spirituality in society it is necessary to maintain societal pressure or repudiate hard-won democracy. I am far removed from such sentiments, as are you, I assume.

But where then is the paradox, when nothing interests us any more, when we live, excuse me, like gypsies these days? But this is a very bad example, for gypsies are apparently freer than you and me. I had in mind the fact that we don't think about tomorrow. If it interested us, we would not have our current lifestyle. Life has escaped our control—even in the most democratic of countries in the West. In the end, all of this can't help but have an effect on our culture. And those details, like the crisis of contemporary literature, the contemporary novel, cinema—all of these are already such trifles and trivialities, the completely logi-cal conclusion of the interrelation between our inner life and social condition.

One could say, however, that art has always been in a state of crisis. Moreover, it would be very superficial to maintain that a renaissance in some sort of economic, social sense has continually corresponded with a renaissance in the cultural sphere. Only by vulgarly distorting this sociological idea could one think in such a way. But if we begin to compare a spiritual renaissance with an economic one, we will see disparity and discord. Look at a celebrated reactionary period in Russia, beginning with defeat in the Russian-Japanese War right up to the 1917 Revolution, which was a period of crisis and spiritual degradation. It is well known that this happened to be the last renaissance of Russian culture, and it ended not in 1917 but rather much later, sometime at the end of the twenties. I do not aspire to great precision here, for the intelligentsia studied art, philosophy, and religion in the West. . . . In sum, this is an example that demonstrates one of the arguments against crudely explaining spiritual flights through certain economic successes.

What is occurring with us now? I am searching for the words which will not really offend you. For, naturally, I hold myself up to these same claims. The meaning is in the following: we have lost our spirituality, we have ceased to have any need for it. Why? Let's pause with the simple fact that I posed this question . . . Yet it would seem that this is the wrong time to lose our spirituality. For there has never been such a difficult situation on the planet, be it in a political, spiritual, or social sense.

People can take exception to what I'm claiming—they say that throughout history there have always been difficult periods and intellectuals have always cried that the end of the world is approaching, the Apocalypse is coming, that it's impossible to live, that there's no freedom, and so forth. But at the same time, I can open, for instance, the memoirs of Montaigne who, as is well known, lived at the height of various religious wars in France, when blood was flowing freely, Catholics were slitting the throats of Protestants, when it was impossible to go from one fortress to another without being robbed, when villages and cities burned and gallows stood along roadsides . . . It was impossible to even call this existence, for life wasn't worth a kopeck. And in the face of this, Montaigne wrote that had he been told that, on account of various reasons, he could not live, even if he wanted to, in one of the Far Indies, he would consider himself seriously offended. From the point of view of contemporary man's situation, this is simply ridiculous. For it is ridiculous to complain about such a thing since many people live not only without the opportunity to travel to one of the Far Indies but also often without the ability to move from one city to another in one's own country.

In short, why do I speak of this? Because, regardless of the fact that exclamations about the end of the world and crises have arisen for a long time, humans have never experienced the degree of pressure that we experience today. And the paradox, it would seem, is that it is specifically now that it is necessary for artists to approach their own profession and their own selves in a completely different way. But, nevertheless, we see that art is in a very difficult situation and only produces ordinary goods.

This is the relatively gloomy picture that arises before me when I think about the problems of contemporary art. I believe, however, that an enormous task has been entrusted to art. This is the task of resurrecting spirituality. What, we might ask, is realism in the most general sense of the word, as it is known in the West and elsewhere? Created in the flow of this realism are great works of Pushkin, Shakespeare, Tolstoy, Dickens, and so forth, names familiar to everyone. Realism constitutes the truth of humankind.

We can easily become void of the spiritual, for we almost are. But artists acknowledging this spiritual crisis should themselves aspire to spirituality. It is impossible to attach the label of realism to art that speaks about humans by only describing their material form. We're now speaking of a certain loss of spirituality, but we nevertheless speak of spirituality! Recently in conversation about a certain Italian painter I asked, "What does this work signify? It lacks any sort of spiritual content. This is pure superficiality! It is missing what is most important—the inner essence of mankind." And it is exactly the predominant lack of spirituality expressed here that is itself the monument—the exclamation mark for our dearth of spirituality. This is essentially the peril that this artist is screaming about. . . . But this is almost illiterate in form, for in order to demonstrate our lack of spirituality and the drama of this, we must look at a human being within whom the moral hole is gaping.

This type of image can only be created by an artist working on a spiritual plane. In one of Hemingway's novels, *A Farewell to Arms* I think, when the hero says farewell to the body of his deceased wife, the

American writer describes how emptiness emerged in the spot where the hero's heart once was. In all, this is only one image, but it lets the reader imagine the sense of inner struggle. He could describe the outward behavior of the hero but this wouldn't be sufficient.

I think the time has come to say exactly what I have in mind when I use the word "spirituality." For we have already been accustomed to this word, but it is sufficiently abstract when speaking of spirituality's presence in art work. With the word "spirituality" I first of all have in mind a person's interest in what has been called the meaning of life. This is the first step, at least. People who ask themselves this question can no longer sink below this level. They will develop and move onward. What do we live for? Where are we going? What is the meaning of our presence on this planet over the course of—we will flatter one another—the eighty years or so that we live on the Earth? The people who do not ask themselves these questions or have not yet asked them are individuals without spirituality. In other words, they exist on the level of animals, felines—animals don't ask themselves such questions.

I won't deny that I have seen very happy cats. I especially like Kipling's. But in this case how does a person differ from an animal? Is there really a difference? Perhaps we are simply highly developed animals, as I was taught, in fact, for many years. We are different from animals in that we are conscious of ourselves. What does this imply? We see ourselves at the center of the world. We sense that we are at the center of the universe. It would seem that we are aware of this and sense it, but for some reason we have ceased to be amazed by this phenomenon.

So far as we have asked ourselves the question of why we live, we also demand an answer to it. And the artist who is not preoccupied with this question is not an artist. He is not a realist for he disregards one of the most crucial problems, a problem that makes humans true humans, unlike animals. And it is when we begin to take on these questions that what we call true art arises.

It seems to me that I possess sufficient artistic taste, if only because I studied for many years at an art school. I say this only so that you can understand that I have the right to judge pictorial art from almost a professional point of view. So therefore I should note that pictorial art of the twentieth century, even in its highest manifestations and accomplishments, lacks spirituality and is thus flawed. The searching of contemporary artists is focused on certain external issues. And all these searches for style and desire to belong to some sort of school are only for the sake of showing one's work and selling one's work. When we recall the work of Leonardo, when we recall, I don't know, Piero della Francesca, when we think of Roublev (please forgive me, for I can count and count those artists whom I eternally love), when we remember Rembrandt—before us arises a colossal inner human world, intense and powerful. In short, there is the impression that even the celebrated and masterful Picasso did not bother with the question of where we are going and why we exist, and don't try proving me wrong here, because Picasso took on entirely different questions.

Picasso, regardless of his unrivaled mastery, does not conform to my tastes at all. Who would say that he is a spiritual artist who sensed the drama of contemporary humans? He searched for harmony in the world's disharmony, but he did not find it. For his insignia is his fragmentation. He painted many of his canvases as well as entire periods with the same model, the same pattern, turning it around in various shades of light and various levels of foreshortening, as if he wanted to capture the inner presence of man in this world, as if he was following the rhythm of life. He was a sociologist through and through, but he was not spiritual.

Let's recall the French artist Henri Rousseau who worked in the "naïve" style, and let's try and recall the many contemporary artists who try to paint in this manner. You'll see an enormous difference! All that remains is a style, while an interior world ceases to interest anyone. When we meet we are not interested in talking about what we're thinking about and what we live for. We want to look at one another, touch one another, drink together, dance, have sex, but heaven forbid unsettle one another. Parting, we don't want to trouble one another. This is socially dictated indifference. All of it finds its reflection in art. But here's the paradox: depicting this, artists themselves lose their spirituality.

Not long ago in one book, written by Il'in, a well-known Russian philosopher, theosophist, anthroposophist, and a man who studied culture and aesthetics, I read a very strange thing about how artists, poets, geniuses all create their own people. That is, they provide their people with a spiritual sense, as if spiritualizing them. Despite several very perceptive observations made in this book, I find it impossible to concur with Il'in. My observations point to the opposite, that an artist constitutes the voice of the people and expresses their inner, spiritual state by means of language, thereby conveying the feelings, thoughts, and hopes of the people who in an aesthetic sense are silent. I cannot explain this phenomenon in any other way, for society's current spiritual state noticeably weighs upon the artist.

Hence, I believe that there is only one path, and regardless of whether it is good or bad, there is no alternative: artists must be true to their talent and must attempt to explain for themselves why they live. And they must distinguish certain vitally important ideals, spiritual and ethical ideals that help them and the people to develop spiritually. Why do contemporary artists want quick reimbursement for what they do? Not that long ago, approximately a hundred years ago, artists believed that they should simply work, and that their fate was decided by God's will and not for them to worry about. Today artists immediately demand payment in return for their work. As never before! Even Chaliapin in his time said that only birds sing for free. Perhaps I'm taking this out of context, but it seems to me that it is difficult to discuss the spirituality of an artist who makes such pronouncements. On the other hand, however, artists have never been so horrendously provided for as they are now.

Let's take, for instance, the art of the nineteenth century produced by the Russian nobility. Everyone knows, of course, the difficult life that Dostoevsky led, but many other famous writers such as Tolstoy, Leskov, Turgenev, and many others, lived and worked remarkably well on their estates. In short, artists used to be freer to choose a spiritual path. Under the current democracy of our country, artists find themselves in a situation where they are often impelled to work for mere handouts. And nevertheless, as Andre Breton stated in his Surrealist Manifesto, the question of food and earnings can not explain why artists turn into prostitutes. In each case artists are responsible for their fate. But the problem persists. And the results of such a state of affairs are, in general, present for everyone to see.

Yet, I repeat, in my opinion the problem of art's current situation depends in large part on the artists themselves. And we shouldn't have to await remuneration or prosperity if we want to remain artists.

This is essentially the spectrum of questions that worry me more than anything else. Of course, this is one aspect of what we might call the responsibility of the artist. But there are also other aspects.

Humans have been created in the likeness of God, and if we carry within ourselves an artistic seed—every person inherently carries it within them—then we should not squander our talent, for we do not have the right to consider it our own property. We need to remember this if we want to remain cognizant of the demands that are presented to artists. Perhaps from the outside this looks like a conflict, like a standoff between the artist and the public. But we ought to serve, not paying any attention to anyone or anything, regardless of differing tastes, interests, and wishes. For if we don't forget the reason why we are here then this will, for the most part, cease to be abhorrent, for the artist is the voice of the people—even when the artist vociferously denies this. This then is essentially the point of my conversation with you today. I perhaps overlooked something that still remains unclear, even from the perspective of this specific topic.

But in that case I am ready to answer any questions that you might have . . .

Q: *I understand quite well what Mr. Tarkovsky has spoken about so honestly and the problems that confront him presently. The public comprehends quite clearly that you want to utter a "spiritual" word. But what I want to ask you is whether you think the public's reaction bothers you and whether the public has understood this "spiritual" word?*
T: Well, first of all, when I spoke, I did not have the aim of rousing your spirituality. For I, like every one of you, work in my own sphere. I am not a preacher who wants to achieve a quick reaction from the public. I do not possess this ability. For this requires a special sort of ability and talent to which I do not aspire. Therefore I cannot count on you leaving this hall with an aura over your head, and that, having been transformed, you can commence an entirely new life. My task has consisted in helping people understand one another better. It has been important for me that my viewers know my professional problems, those that bother me most of all.

So if you were to ask me whether I calculate the spiritual effect that occurs in viewers when they watch my films, I would at least admit that this is an important question requiring a significant answer from me. But since you did not ask this question, I won't answer it. But my aim in today's conversation has been in a certain way to come into contact with you so that you might better understand me and to share, as if with other professionals, my own personal problems. And I will be very happy if at some level these issues have occupied your mind.

Q: *Can you define this question of spirituality more precisely? Does this presuppose for you an attitude toward the Creator and the divine? And have you arrived at some sort of answer, or, as an artist, do you only pose this question to yourself?*

T: It seems to me that I am inherently a very simple person, and therefore in no way can I agree with the elementary thought that it is simpler, for instance, to believe in the idea that the world always existed than to think that in this casual world there exists a cause which appeared prior to the creation of all matter. And when they try to convince me that there is no such reason for my presence on this earth, forgive me, but I cannot believe this. It is too idealistic, but please forgive me for this paradox.

In regards to defining my system of spirituality more precisely, I have already said that I pose myself this question about the meaning of life and then I try to answer it. And it is for the sake of this question that I work. I try to create a model that can explain what my ideals are, especially in the context of what I see as the striving of humans and our reason for living. It seems to me that I have already spoken sufficiently about the first step in judging one's own spirituality. For if we are going to talk in general about the problems of spirituality, then we lack something in life. In fact, quite a number of people, completing their life's journey, not only are unable to answer this question, but have never even asked themselves the question.

Q: *Why is it specifically in our time that the public demands art lacking in spirituality?*

T: The public does not demand art that lacks spirituality. In general it doesn't demand any sort of art. Of course, there will always be viewers who are interested in true art. But I am talking about the public upon which the artist's commercial well-being is based. It accordingly doesn't demand any sort of art; rather it demands entertainment.

Q: *Does it bother you that you can lose spirituality, losing that which appeared so prominently in your film* The Mirror?

T: This question is a very serious one, no doubt a serious one. When we speak of the loss of spirituality, in a certain social sense, this does not mean that someone personally loses spirituality, like losing one's money or depleting one's bank account. This process expresses itself in a different way: people are being born without any bank account. They somehow survive without it. They are raised and educated in a different way. This society loses its spirituality, but not some specific individual.

For if—certainly "if" in this case—somebody is at a certain spiritual level, he cannot lose it. If, that is, he does not commit some mortal sin or mistake as, for instance, happened with Raskolnikov. And the most horrible thing for a person who senses that they are at a certain spiritual level is to lose it. *Hamlet* is about this very issue. In order not to break away from life, in order to live so as to be connected materially with this world, the Danish Prince had to lower himself to the level of the villains who lived around him in Elsinore. The tragedy is not in the fact that he dies, since death for him is an escape from his situation, but in the fact that although a spiritual man he becomes a murderer. This is a tragedy of the spirit. With this his tragedy differs for instance from ancient tragedy.

Q: *You spoke about the situation of the Western artist. But could you please describe the situation and condition of the artist in Eastern Europe? If the Western artist lives in a spiritual wasteland, then what is happening with the Eastern artist?*

T: I can't answer that. More accurately, I can only use myself as an example, for I can't speak about other people. Because, for instance, I will mention someone and then in some newspaper a response will appear, written by this very person, in which he will declare that I'm deceiving my Western audience. Therefore, as I said, I will only talk about myself.

In terms of a lack of spirituality in the West, I wouldn't generalize in that way. By talking about this in such general terms, you yourself juxtapose the lack of spirituality here in the West with the spirituality there in the East. But all of this is not so absolute. I will not deny that here in the West I have met and continue to meet an enormous number of people who are spiritually rich, but I am speaking about a general tradition, about a tendency within which society develops. I would never be so bold as to claim that Western society is absolutely void of spirituality while Eastern European society is spiritual. This would simply not be true. Yet this tendency does exist. The sense of a certain spiritual wasteland, of a certain public isolation exists here, while a sense of unity with the people and a spiritual dependence on the people exists for us. I have no doubt about this. If we were to talk specifically about my situation, then everything about me is more or less well known. I do not want to take up your time. Even on those pamphlets that were handed out right before our gathering, so much has been written about me, including sufficient information to answer your question.

Q: *We really don't need to learn about your spirituality, for we can sense it in your films.*
T: Then I don't completely understand what they want from me . . .

Q: *Perhaps Mr. Tarkovsky can say a few words about Sergei Paradjanov?*
T: When I left the Soviet Union, Sergei Paradjanov had just been released from prison and his subsequent fate was still unknown. From what I have heard in the West, he just made a picture in Tblisi at "Georgia-Film," and they say that the film is a success. The medieval history of a certain fortress in Georgia is the basis for this film. I have not seen the film, but I hope to. I heard it was accepted almost without any edits. Sergei Paradjanov is now preparing for his next production. I don't know however what it will be.

Q: *You spoke about spiritual development and the loss of spirituality, but can you really develop spiritually? Either it exists or it doesn't.*
T: I find it strange to field such a question. You probably need to talk to people who have devoted their whole lives to the question of spiritual development. Millions of books have been written about this. In various parts of the world and at various points of history. Therefore I'll have to point you toward these books. But if you are expecting an

answer from me, then the entire point of human existence consists in using the time allotted to you to take at least one step away from the level upon which you were born up to a higher level. This is the meaning of life.

Q: *Andrei Arsen'evich, I have two questions for you. The first question is whether you consider yourself a person of faith who follows the teachings of the Russian Orthodox Church? And my second question concerns the views which you so eloquently put forth today and how they are so reminiscent of various views held by Orthodox thinkers of the previous century, especially Khomyakov and Dostoevsky. Isn't it true that in your case this is most likely a reaction to Soviet propaganda and the Soviet worldview, rather than a rejection of the Western world?*

T: What does the Western world have to do with this? In terms of my inner problems, I can both talk and not talk about them. I consider myself a person of faith, but I do not want to delve into the nuances and problems of my situation, for it is not so straightforward, not so simple, and not so unambiguous. For now let's not talk so much about my views, but rather about Slavophilism. I like how you lumped Khomyakov and Dostoevsky together. For this already is an answer to your question, since Dostoevsky was not a Slavophile. He was even an opponent of Khomyakov and parted company in many ways. Dostoevsky was too great to meddle in some certain "movement" or to even belong to a "movement." He said and wrote this word in quotation marks.

   I am far removed from the views of Slavophiles. In this sense I agree with Solzhenitsyn in a lot of ways. In terms of my attitude toward the West, I gather that you are talking about my reaction to what I see in the West, how I judge everything, and naturally, how I respond as an individual. Since I was educated in the Soviet Union, my reaction cannot help but depend on my education. In general, everything is entirely natural: I am who I am. And my inner essence determines my reactions. But for me the question lies elsewhere. Having remained in the West for a long time, would I resign myself to this point of view, would I resign myself to this situation, or would my sensibility become even deeper and more dramatic? It is very difficult to answer this now. But . . . let's see. If we do live long enough to notice a certain difference, then we will talk about this topic.

You probably noticed that I am not that inclined to criticize the country in which I lived for some fifty odd years. I don't belong to that group of people who immediately begin to clip coupons, zealously criticizing something and extolling something else. This question of the interrelation of two worlds is incredibly important. I would even say vitally important. This is not simply a problem of coexistence, for one could be even more catastrophic and exclamatory in describing it. I'm keeping away from any hasty conclusions. These ideas and problems have my constant attention. And I think about them all the time. But I don't want to talk about them right now, because it is too premature.

There are things that interest me much more than politics, although, of course, there are social conflicts and problems that certainly worry me as an artist. We trust politicians and parties so much that professional politicians determine everything for us now. Sometime ago, belonging to a party was not any sort of professional mark, but now party membership is already a profession! But in general this doesn't interest me. Because from start to finish it is terribly flawed. The Grand Inquisitor came, took away your free will, offered you either a piece of bread or democracy, and said: I will worry about this, and you will concern yourself with that. . . . In short, there are professional leaders who guide us toward prosperity, who lead us to the brink of catastrophe, and then there are people who imagine that this path is true and therefore wholeheartedly trust the leaders. Here is the price we pay, either for a piece of bread or for what has been called Western European democracy.

I don't want to delve too deep here, I only want to direct your attention to the fact that all this strikes me as insanely false. But Dostoevsky has already written about this. We really don't read Dostoevsky. Forgive me for talking about Dostoevsky, but I am Russian and I love Dostoevsky. One can name other people, no less significant, who have made their impact on world culture, on the West and elsewhere, but it turns out that Dostoevsky is more relevant here. Therefore, when you say that I am criticizing something or don't understand something, it is that I don't acknowledge what I believe everyone should resist acknowledging: how it is possible to entrust your soul to someone else and to live happily without a soul, like a slightly crazed person in an insane asylum . . .

Q: *Still one last question. You have mentioned that Western art is focused on itself and egocentric. But if one asked, who is the director who thinks most of all about his own soul, about his own personal problems, and his own childhood, one would have to say it is Tarkovsky. It seems that you have this very same self-fixation. You evidently make a distinction between self-reflection and self-absorption? Where do you draw this line?*

T: Don't you understand that I deal with Western culture like any Russian, like Dostoevsky did, like all Russian culture? You want to excuse me of egocentrism, but I have never repudiated it. You said that I am egocentric in my work; I not only don't deny this, I even admit that this is my credo. This is not a reproach, this is a fact. I am clearly talking about the difference between Eastern and Western spirituality. And I did not say that I myself am situated somewhere over there in the East. I am quite far removed, let's say, from what a certain Japanese painter once did: Having earned his name and glory in the court of a Shogun, a Japanese feudal lord, the painter abandoned everything, left for another place where no one knew him, and began a new career under a different name. He even developed a new style. All of this is completely impossible in the West, and I am a bit envious of it. We're not at all like this.

Q: *With this we bring to an end the question period, but would you like to say something in conclusion, Andrei?*

T: I finished my last speech with what I also want to say now. I didn't come here with the aim of appearing like a prophet of spirituality, especially before an audience whose spirituality might be higher than my own. I simply wanted to focus your attention on the issue, without which art has never and could never exist. But today it is so often the case that what we call art has never really, in its essence, been art. And to a much greater degree than we think. This is what I wanted to focus your attention on. Otherwise we will soon begin to feed off of things that really weren't meant to be eaten, even if simply out of disgust.

Red Tape

A N G U S   M A c K I N N O N / 1 9 8 4

IN THE EARLY HOURS OF TUESDAY, July 10, 1984, Andrei Tarkovsky took perhaps the most difficult and momentous decision of his life. Speaking at a press conference in Milan, the fifty-two-year-old Russian film director explained that the Soviet authorities had not replied to any of the letters he had written requesting permission to extend his working stay in the West, and had offered him no guarantees of employment were he to return to the Soviet Union. Similarly, there had been no official reply to his demands that his aging, ill mother-in-law and young son Andrei be allowed to join him and his wife Larissa in Italy where he had been living since completing his last film, *Nostalgia*. As a result, Tarkovsky, the Soviet Union's most remarkable contemporary filmmaker and, ironically, also its most indisputably Russian, found himself compelled to seek asylum in the West and go into reluctant exile.

Tarkovksy has aged visibly in the nine months since I first met him; the flesh of his face seems to crease itself even more tightly over the prominent bone structure, exaggerating his every expression, and the streaks of grey in his jet-black hair are more numerous. Yet Tarkovsky, a slight, bashful man whose hands are forever scratching his head, brushing back his hair, tugging at his moustache or an ear, gesturing expansively, appears markedly more at ease. And when he smiles or laughs self-deprecatingly at something he has said, his face relaxes instantly, his eyes bright as a bird's.

From *Time Out* (London), 9–15 August 1984, 20–22. Reprinted by permission.

Although he still cannot speak as frankly as he would perhaps like, Tarkovsky doesn't hesitate to itemize his grievances, to explain why, after years of being "chased as a deer by dogs" by the state film organization Goskino, he took the irrevocable decision to leave the USSR.

Two and a half years ago Tarkovsky was given permission to work abroad, in Italy, on *Nostalgia*, a film primarily concerned with the Russian's inability to live outside Russia for any length of time. The completed film was scheduled to be shown at the 1983 Cannes Festival, but Tarkovsky was "amazed" to discover Goskino were insisting that actor, director (*War and Peace, Waterloo*), and epitome of Soviet cinematic orthodoxy, Sergei Bondarchuk represent the USSR on the festival's jury panel.

"I was," Tarkovsky says, "so surprised because I know that Bondarchuk can't bear me, can't tolerate me in any way—his expression changes the moment he sees me. So I telephoned Moscow to ask why they were sending someone who definitely doesn't wish me any good at all." Tarkovsky was told that Bondarchuk had talked extensively with Filip Yermash, the minister of cinematography, and was now resolved to offer Tarkovsky unqualified support and to do his utmost to keep the bourgeois Western critics at bay.

Full of foreboding, Tarkovsky went to Cannes and could only look on appalled as Bondarchuk fought "like a tiger" against the other jury members who were determined to give *Nostalgia* an award, and "did everything he could to discredit me and my picture." As it was, the jury nonetheless awarded *Nostalgia* a Grand Prix for Creative Cinema—but the damage was done and, as far as Tarkovsky was concerned, irreparable.

"Bondarchuk's behavior made me understand that this very negative attitude was the official position of Goskino. And that was a terrible blow for me. It was betrayal. It was a knife into my back. This was after all a film in which I tried to express the impossibility for a Russian to live abroad, how Russians feel lonely and alone in the West. Goskino rejected a film which was made from a very clear position of a Russian citizen . . . I still can't understand it. I was shattered and I understood that if I went back to Moscow straightaway, I would never have any work again."

Instead, Tarkovsky embarked upon what was to prove a fruitless attempt to extract an explanation from Goskino and the Soviet authorities. He wrote to Yermash, setting out his case, to the head of the cultural department of the Party's Central Committee, twice to Andropov, then to Chernenko. The silence was deafening, and when Yermash eventually gave him verbal assurances that if he were to return to Moscow, "everything could be sorted out," Tarkovsky was in no mood to acquiesce: "I couldn't trust one word he says, he is false through and through. I have no doubt now that it was a calculated game to keep me outside the borders of Soviet art. In all my letters I told them that if I received no answer, I would have to take the next step, which I just wouldn't want to do. But the last blow was that I never expected my *government* would not answer me, would pretend that I didn't exist . . .

"I cannot understand this," Tarkovsky insists earnestly. "Bondarchuk, even Yermash, who was I think under great pressure from my colleagues, I can understand all this, not to forgive but . . . but my government—all my films were sold abroad to earn hard currency, I was of quite considerable use to the state, I was trying to increase the glory of Soviet cinema. But my films never got Soviet awards, were never shown at Soviet film festivals. . . . And yet I have never been a dissident, I always considered myself a poet (like his father, Arseni Tarkovsky). I'm talking about my rights; all I wanted to do was make films, and yet I have only been allowed to make five in twenty years . . ."

Tarkovsky turns abruptly in his chair, his combined agitation and incomprehension forcing him to pause, stares through the French window. Fascinated, he watches a dandelion clock drift lethargically to the ground, a coruscating orb of light, before he begins to relate a depressing catalogue of what he euphemistically describes as "difficulties."

Andrei Roublev (1968), Tarkovsky's epic treatment of the life of the fifteenth-century icon painter, was named as an "outstanding work of art" by a special Goskino committee and chosen to represent the USSR at Cannes. But the film was still removed from the plane at Moscow airport an hour before take-off—and shelved for almost six years. A celebrated Soviet filmmaker, whom Tarkovsky won't name, had apparently complained to the Central Committee that *Roublev* was "anti-historical, anti-Russian, a film full of anti's," and as a result Tarkovsky found himself without work, his every submitted project refused: "They took these years from my life. No one apologized when they finally gave *Roublev* a very limited release. I was told I had to thank everyone instead."

The largely autobiographical *The Mirror* (1974) received similarly summary treatment: special screenings in Moscow to cater for unprecedented ticket demand were cancelled on the pretext of their coinciding with official celebrations, after which the film was never shown again. And so on and so forth—even if Tarkovsky's films were given nominal distribution, they were often poor black and white copies of painstakingly tinted color originals while, more disturbingly, each print carried with it an official disclaimer, indicating that it was "prohibited, not to be advertised in any way."

Tarkovsky remains genuinely baffled by the hostility his films succeeded in arousing. When I suggest that his work might at times have been construed as too metaphysical, mystical even, by a Soviet film industry weened on "materialistic realism," he shrugs before declaring that the only argument consistently advanced against his work was not primarily ideological, but simply that Russian audiences did not want to see his films—an argument directly contradicted by his own experience when introducing his work to the public in the Soviet Union, by his conversations with distributors desperate to acquire his films, and by the newspaper *Kosolomoskaya Pravda*'s unsolicited assertion that *Stalker* (1979) was one of the USSR's six most commercially successful films.

"The argument is always the same," Tarkovsky comments, "is now being repeated like parrots by Soviet directors when they visit the West—that I make films for the elite. But this lie is so obvious it's clear there are no true arguments against me. If I do make films for the elite, then I am very happy the elite in the Soviet Union is so big, counts so many thousands.

"But it seems that there exists just some sort of *zoological* hatred towards me on the part of my colleagues in high positions, the film directors as well as the bureaucrats . . . I don't know why."

And did anyone actually help him while he was being morally and financially supported by his wife, herself an assistant film director at Mosfilm, through the years when he was effectively prevented from working and, as he puts it, "many, many obstacles were put in my way"?

"There were two or three people who treated me with great warmth, but nominally. They expressed their compassion, but they didn't really help. I don't even want to name them, because it may cause problems. . . . I could, you know, have put up with even more difficulties—and but for my wife I wouldn't have coped with any of it—but I just couldn't accept the villainy when the authorities turned away from me at the most difficult time of my life. This was more than I could bear . . ."

Tarkovsky's main concern now is for his mother-in-law and son, who will be fourteen on August 7 ("Andrei asks," Tarkovsky's interpreter explains, "if you can perhaps wish his son happy birthday from him through your magazine"). "We are about to send an invitation to them because, according to both international and Soviet law, families must be preserved and so I count on seeing them soon." At present, he has not been officially stripped of his Soviet citizenship, but admits that it is only a matter of time. Meanwhile, his application for asylum is being processed, although to which country he understandably declines to say.

Tarkovsky is resigned to his predicament, describing it as "the drama, the tragedy of many who are compelled to leave the Soviet Union." The USSR's reluctance to abide by the Helsinki Agreement and guarantee freedom of travel out of and back into the Soviet Union he considers "a terrible, a horrifying mistake . . . if the government followed the Agreement, I'm sure almost everybody would go back. I personally can't imagine how I'm going to live here. I really can't say whether I will be able to cope, to know whether I will be able to pull myself together after all this is over."

As for his work, Tarkovsky is not so uncertain: "It's absolutely clear now that my work will take on a new character, and I think this break is noticeable even in *Nostalgia*. My previous pictures were a creative act for me; I made them as a professional filmmaker and I separated my films from myself. *Nostalgia* on the other hand is an exact reprint of my state of mind; it was my deed. I really wouldn't want to watch it again—it would be the same as someone who is ill looking at an x-ray of their illness."

Nonetheless, Tarkovsky wasn't even remotely contemplating staying in the West while making *Nostalgia*: "This was furthest from my mind. But when I saw the film for the first time from start to finish, I got very frightened. The film had been creating the situation, was almost making *me*, I don't know what I was doing." Although *Nostalgia* did succeed in transplanting Tarkovsky's highly idiosyncratic vision to Italy: "Yes, the stylistic unity, the world I am trying to express—it is my world, and I don't doubt that whether I am filming in Africa or China, it will be clear that the film is made by a Russian artist. This is a natural thing; if it weren't so, it would just prove that I don't exist, that what exist are some external circumstances which I as a film director organize. . . . One can divide filmmakers into two categories: those who express their private world and those who try to reconstruct what they see around themselves—and I belong to the first category."

In fact, the first of Tarkovsky's many planned projects will be *The Sacrifice*; the film will be made for the Swedish Film Institute, be shot on the Swedish island of Gotland and will star Erland Josephson, who played the reclusive Domenico in *Nostalgia*.

"I look forward to work in Sweden now because I found an amazingly beautiful place. It gives the impression of complete emptiness, it's so empty (*laughs*) and flat I doubt whether I have the right to film there, and all the time I'm afraid I won't have sufficient things, materials that I can use there. But in principle it's good because that's exactly what I've been aiming at—the dream of any artist is to use minimal means, because we are created in the image of God and share this creativity with God. That is all we need. Usually, you see, you have more than you need, more material things, and that's worse than not having enough."

The central character of *The Sacrifice* will be a former actor who now writes about the arts and "his inner, personal responsibility for every-thing that's going on in the world, and how he takes the weight of guilt or the blame for it all, giving up his happiness in order to save everyone . . ." Like Domenico in *Nostalgia*? "Yes, a little, only this time he really is going to save everyone." From what, an apocalypse? "A war, a nuclear one—although nuclear war and the Apocalypse are almost the same now and it is possible that such a war will turn into the Apocalypse we read about in Revelation, even into something much worse . . .

"If mankind," Tarkovsky continues apace, warming to a favorite theme, "gets prepared, it is possible to head off the Apocalypse, but per-sonally I don't have any belief that mankind wants to get ready. Modern man negates it all. Yes, I am talking about a spiritual crisis: the lack of spirituality in the world needs to be opposed and so the Apocalypse itself is, so to speak, creating a spiritual balance . . ." By its imminence? "Yes," Tarkovsky replies emphatically, smiling all the while.

Talk of the spiritual dimension of modern life prompts me to quote something *Le Monde* reported Tarkovsky as saying about the West lacking this dimension. "What I meant was that the everyday welfare, peace, and well-being in the West, this material satisfaction provides the reason for a European to become a conformist, makes him want to keep the things he's got. This 'lukewarm' state is something St. John talks about in his 'Apocalypse'—he says it is better that you are either hot or cold rather than lukewarm . . .

"But, God forbid," Tarkovsky qualifies, "I'm not accusing anyone of anything. I don't know enough about the West, although in a spiritual sense the atmosphere here is a bit difficult to breathe, as in outer space or high up in the mountains. It doesn't mean that to make society spiritual you have to have terrible pressure from above—that's crazy—but I have noticed that somehow the way people communicate with each other is different here than in Russia.

"In Russia when people meet it brings joy, it's a reward, and people are very grateful to each other . . . but here there seems to be a wish to separate, to fence oneself off. But Italy I love very much, it's a very special country; people are so communicative there—Fellini expresses this in his pictures very well.

"At the moment, though, I feel a little cut-off myself, I think of my loved ones with whom I am out of touch. In fact I don't like the noise of big cities too much. If I had the choice, I would live in a village all my life." And Tarkovsky shrugs again, then laughs with pleasure at the thought.

Whether or not Andrei Tarkovsky will be able to accept what he sees as his enforced exile, to continue to express the creativity he regards as God-given, remains to be seen. The chances, one suspects, are that he will, despite his own misgivings: his determinedly metaphysical view of the world stems from and is buttressed by a religious faith of extraordinary tenacity. And although the more cynical may dismiss Tarkovsky's remarkably ungrudging pride in his country and its achievements as misplaced, naive in the extreme, they forget the strength of feeling of Russians whose lives were in any way affected by the Great Patriotic War against Nazi Germany. Whatever else he may lose, Tarkovsky will not lose that loyalty, in its fashion another kind of faith.

Similarly, Tarkovsky cannot be dismissed as an anachronism. On the contrary, his aesthetic, the breathtaking lyricism and resonance of his work are all directly descended from a Russian artistic tradition whose greatest practitioners the Revolution has posthumously canonized while at the same time making every effort to ensure that the tradition itself cannot be perpetuated. And that—the temporary triumph of bureaucracy driven fearfully into uncomprehending vindictiveness when confronted by the visionary—is as much of a tragedy as Tarkovsky's own.

Portrait of a Filmmaker as a Monk-Poet

LAURENCE COSSÉ / 1986

Ivan's Childhood

Q: *How did you choose the subject of your first film,* Ivan's Childhood?
T: The story of this film is a bit strange. Mosfilm studios started the production of *Ivan's Childhood* with another director, other actors, a different crew. More than half the film was shot by this crew, half the budget was spent, but the result was so bad that Mosfilm decided to stop the production. The administration then looked for another director, asking well-known directors first, and then lesser known ones. All of them refused to pick up the film. As for me, I had just finished my studies at VGIK and was finishing up my thesis film, *The Steamroller and the Violin.* Before accepting the proposal, I put forth several conditions. I wanted to read the novel of Vladimir Bogomolov, from which the screenplay had been taken, once more, in order to re-write the screenplay completely; I refused to look at even one foot of what had previously been shot; and finally, I demanded that the entire cast and crew be replaced, in order to start over from scratch. "Okay," I was told, "but you will only have half of the budget!"—"If you let me do what I want, I accept a half-budget," I replied. This is how the film got made.

Q: Ivan's Childhood *is, then, a film entirely born of Andrei Tarkovsky, except for the subject?*
T: That's right.

From a broadcast on *France-Culture*, January 7, 1986. Reprinted by permission. Translated from French by Susana Rossberg.

Q: *But this subject is also very close to you. The young Ivan is as old as the young Andrei Tarkovsky during the war.*

T: My childhood was very different from that of Ivan who experienced the war as an adult, and as a combatant. All Russian boys my age, however, had a very difficult life. To say that something links Andrei Tarkovsky to Ivan is to remind us of the community of suffering established between Ivan and all young Russians of this generation.

Q: *When it was presented in Venice in 1962, the film was perceived as a profound reflection on war, on history . . .*

T: The film was certainly very well received, but it remained completely misunderstood by the critics. Each one interpreted the story, the narrative, the characters of the film, whereas it was the first work of a young director, therefore a poetic work to be understood from my point of view, not from the historical point of view. Sartre, for instance, ardently defended the film against the criticism of the Italian Left, but strictly from a philosophical point of view. As far as I'm concerned that wasn't a valid defense. I was looking for an artistic, not an ideological defense. I'm not a philosopher, I'm an artist. From my point of view, his defense was totally useless. He was trying to evaluate the film using his own philosophical values, and I, Andrei Tarkovsky, artist, was put aside. One spoke only about Sartre, and no longer about the artist.

Q: *Sartre's interpretation of* Ivan's Childhood—*that war produces monsters and devours heros—isn't yours?*

T: I do not dispute the interpretation. I completely agree with this vision: war produces hero-victims. There is no winner in a war. When one wins a war, one loses it at the same time. I do not dispute the interpretation, but the framework of this polemic: ideas, values were stressed, art and the artist were forgotten.

Andrei Roublev

Q: *How was* Andrei Roublev *born?*

T: Very simply. We were talking with Konchalovsky and another friend over drinks one evening. This friend said, "Why not make a film about Roublev? I'm an actor, I could play Roublev. . . . Ancient Russia, the icons, this would make a good subject . . ." At first this idea seemed to me to be unfeasible, even detestable, too distant from my universe. The next morning however I decided to make this film and, along with Andrei Konchalovsky, we started to think about it. That is how the project developed. Fortunately very little is known about Roublev's life, and that gave us complete freedom of movement, a freedom which was of prime importance to me.

Q: *All the episodes, from the looting of Vladimir to the casting of the bell, were chosen and conceived by you?*
T: All of that was made up. But, before making it up, we of course did a lot of research, we read a lot. In a manner of speaking we invented the life of Andrei Roublev, within the historical limits we had.

Q: *It thus became a very personal film . . .*
T: I don't think I ever made a film that wasn't personal.

Q: *But the film's central question, this creator overwhelmed by evil, who renounces his creation, is that an idea of Tarkovsky's?*
T: Of course. We have no documents about Roublev, besides a couple of his icons. In his career, however, there was a gap, an important moment without evidence of creation. I decided to interpret that as a refusal, but I would be neither surprised nor shocked by another interpretation that would prove, for instance, that during that time Roublev was in Venice. Maybe he wasn't at all disturbed by the destruction of the Vladimir cathedral. I constructed one Roublev, but I would accept other versions.

Q: Andrei Roublev *is a film about the legitimacy of art in a world which is prey to evil. Why create beauty when there is evil everywhere?*
T: The more there is evil in the world, the more we have reasons to create beauty. It is doubtless harder, but it is also more necessary.

Q: *Under the condition that it's not any kind of art?*
T: What does "any kind of art" mean?

Q: *An art that coincides with God's project for the world?*

T: As long as man shall exist, there will be an instinctive tendency for creation. As long as man feels like a man, he will try to create something. Therein lies the link with his Creator. What is creation? What is the use of art? The answer to this question resides in a formula: "art is a prayer." That says it all. Through art, man expresses his hope. Everything that does not express this hope, whatever is not fundamentally spiritual, has nothing to do with art. Otherwise, in the best of cases it'll be but a brilliant intellectual analysis. For instance, the entire Picasso oeuvre is, for me, based on this intellectual analysis. Picasso painted the world in the name of his analysis, of his intellectual reconstruction, and, despite the prestige of his name, I must confess that I don't believe he ever reached art.

Q: *The only art there is postulates that the world has a meaning?*

T: I repeat, art is a form of prayer. Man lives by his prayer alone.

Q: *Many people saw in* Andrei Roublev *a message addressed to the current USSR, for it to recapture the spiritual creativity of the Russia of old.*

T: That's possible, but that really isn't my problem. I'm not sending a message to the current Russia. Moreover, it's no longer my wish to say anything to Russians. I am no longer interested in the virtues of these kind of prophetic stances as "I want to tell my people," "I want to tell the world." I'm not a prophet. I'm a man to whom God gave the possibility of being a poet, meaning, of praying in another manner than the one used by the faithful in a cathedral. I cannot and do not want to say anything more. If Western people see in my films a message directed to the Russian people, that is not my problem, but a problem that should be solved between these two people. Personally, my only concern is to work, only to work.

Solaris

Q: *On the planet Solaris, Kelvin meets his wife, dead for thirty years, once more. Is that the only love story ever told by Tarkovsky, through this impossible relationship?*

T: This love story is one of the aspects of the film. Maybe, indeed, Kelvin's mission on Solaris has only one aim: to show that love of the other is indispensable to all life. A man without love is no longer a man. The entire "solaristic" is meant to show that humanity must be love.

Q: *But this adventure, which at first resembles a science-fiction, is chiefly a spiritual adventure.*
T: It is rather an adventure that happens to one man, within his conscience. I had wanted to direct a film based on Stanislaw Lem's novel, *Solaris*, without making a real cosmic voyage. That would doubtless have been more interesting, but Lem didn't agree.

Q: *What interests Tarkovsky in the cosmos is, however, "the man who spurts out of it," according to your own words. That's also a way of extricating oneself from the cosmic journey.*
T: That is quite true.

Q: *Isn't this cosmos, much like, later on, the Zone of* Stalker, *a metaphor for purgatory, this place where one only desires one thing, to change oneself?*
T: I believe that, even without a purgatory, life revolves entirely around this definition: changing oneself. The only aim of man's life is this change. Purgatory, rather, is necessary in order to calm us, to cool our sufferings down. But I don't exclude the idea that purgatory may be here on earth . . .

The Mirror

Q: The Mirror *reminds the French of the universe of Proust, the universe of memory.*
T: For Proust, time is more than time. For a Russian, all of that isn't a problem. We Russians have to protect ourselves. For Proust, the issue was rather to propagate himself. There is a very strong tradition in Russian literature centered precisely on childhood and adolescent remembrances, on this attempt to settle accounts with one's past, a kind of repentance.

Q: *And was* The Mirror *that? A revival of this literary genre?*
T: Yes. In fact, this film provoked a lot of discussion among Russian spectators. One day, during a public debate organized after a screening,

the discussion dragged on and on. After midnight, a cleaning woman arrived to clean the screening room, wanting to throw us out. She had seen the film earlier on and she didn't understand why we were arguing for such a long time about *The Mirror*. She told us, "Everything is quite simple, someone fell ill and was afraid of dying. He remembered, all of a sudden, all the pain he'd inflicted on others, and he wanted to atone for it, to ask to be pardoned." This simple woman had understood it all, she had grasped the repentance in the film. Russians constantly live with the present time upon them. Literature is made up only of that, and the simple people understand it very well. *The Mirror* is, in that sense, a bit the history of Russians, the history of their repentance. While the critics, present in the screening room, had understood absolutely nothing about the film—and the further things go, the less they understand—this woman who hadn't finished grade school, was telling us the truth in her way, this truth inherent in the Russian people's repertoire.

Stalker

Q: *Who is the Stalker, this mysterious character?*
T: This film tells of a man in pursuit of a quest, but in a very concrete manner. Being idealistic however, he remains a sort of knight fighting for spiritual values. The hero, the Stalker, moves in the same trajectory as Don Quixote or Prince Myshkin, these characters we call "idealists" in novels. It is precisely because they are idealists that they suffer defeats in real life.

Q: *Could we call them "Christ-like characters"?*
T: In a way. For me, they are characters who express the strength of what is weak. This film speaks about man's dependence upon the strength he himself has created. Strength ends up destroying him, and weakness reveals itself as the one and only force.

Q: *What does man do in order to feel this strength of the weak?*
T: That's not what is important. The actions of the man of faith can be totally absurd, not at all rational or thought out. For me, spirituality has always escaped conscious behavior. "Ridiculous," "displaced" actions are a superior form of spirituality.

Q: *That which we call "gratuitous acts."*
T: Yes. However, these acts are not done gratuitously but in order to escape from the world as it exists today, as it has been built up, unable to produce a spiritual man. The important thing, the thing that guides all of Stalker's actions, is this force that leads him away from being common, that renders him ridiculous, idiotic, but that reveals to him his own singularity, his spirituality. This unconscious force is his faith.

Q: *Is the Zone the space of that faith?*
T: I have often been asked what the Zone represents. There is only one answer: the Zone doesn't exist. It's Stalker himself who invented his Zone. He created it in order to take some very unhappy people there, and to impose on them the idea of hope. The chamber of desires is also a Stalker creation, one more provocation in the face of the material world. This provocation, constructed in Stalker's spirit, corresponds to an act of faith.

Nostalghia

Q: *What is the subject of* Nostalghia?
T: The impossibility of living, the absence of freedom. If, for example, one were to establish limits to love, man would become disfigured as a consequence; similarly, if one sets limits to spiritual life, man is traumatized. Some feel it more strongly than others, and attempt to give of themselves completely. They give themselves to others in order to save the world from its lack of love—it's the meaning of sacrifice. When one sees the limits imposed by today's world upon this love, this gift, man must begin to suffer. The hero of *Nostalghia* suffers from the impossibility of being a friend, of being in friendship with everyone. However, he finds a friend who suffers as much as he, the madman, Domenico.

Q: *Is that suffering the nostalgia?*
T: Nostalgia is a complete, total feeling. In other words, one can feel nostalgia while remaining in one's own country, next to those people to whom one is closest. In spite of a happy home, a happy family, man can suffer from nostalgia, simply because he feels his soul is limited, that it cannot propagate itself as he would have wished. Nostalgia is this powerlessness in the face of the world, this pain of being unable to

transmit one's spirituality to other people. It's the illness that overcomes the hero of *Nostalghia*: he suffers from not being able to have
friends, of not being able to communicate with them. This character
says "we must destroy borders" so the entire world can live its spirituality freely, smoothly. He suffers, more generally, because of his character,
unadjusted for modern life. He cannot be happy in the face of the misery of the world. He takes on this collective misery, and wants to live
out of step with the world. His problem is strongly related to compassion. His entire suffering stems from there: he cannot incarnate completely this feeling of compassion. He wants to suffer along with the
rest of mankind, but he doesn't totally succeed at it.

Q: *What remedy could you have given your hero in order to overcome
this suffering?*

T: One must believe in one's sources, in one's roots. Know where one
comes from and where one is going, why one is living. In other words,
to feel constantly one's dependence towards one's Creator. Otherwise, if
the thought of the Creator escapes us, man becomes an animal. Man's
only specificity is his feeling of dependence, this freedom that he gives
himself to feel dependent. This sensation is the path of spirituality.
Man's luck consists in ceaselessly developing the path leading to spirituality. Dependence is man's only chance, since this faith in the
Creator, this humble awareness that one is only the creature of a superior being, this belief has the power to save the world. One must fill
one's life with servitude. This relationship is very simple: it resembles
the one that unites children to a parent. One must recognize the
authority of the other. It is this respect, this servitude, that gives man
the strength to look inside himself, that furnishes him with his intro-
spective, contemplative look. It's this that we call prayer (according to
me, in accordance with Orthodox ritual), but it is equally the form
undertaken by my work in film, my artist's work. I am nonetheless still
far from achieving this ideal prayer.

Q: *Your faith in God thus fuses with your faith in art?*

T: Art is the capacity to create, it's the reflection, the mirror-image, of
the Creator's gesture. We artists only repeat, only imitate that gesture.
Art is one of those precious moments in which we resemble the Creator.

That is why I have never believed in art which would be independent of the supreme Creator, I don't believe in art without God. The raison d'être of art is a prayer, it's my prayer. If this prayer, if my films can bring people to God, so much the better. My life would then take on its sense, the essential sense of "serving." But I would never impose it: to serve does not mean to conquer.

Q: *How can art gravitate toward this objective, "to serve"?*
T: This is where the mystery, like the mystery of Creation, resides. When one kneels down in front of an icon to pray, one finds the right words to express one's love to God, but these words remain secret, mysterious. Likewise, when an artist finds characters, stories, it is as if he prayed. He enters into communion with God in creation, and he finds the right words. That is where the mystery of Creation comes from. Here, art takes on the form of a gift. Art can only "serve" if it is a gift.

Q: *Your films are, therefore, acts of love towards the Creator?*
T: I would like to think so. I'm working on it, in any case. The ideal for me would be to make this constant gift, this gift that Bach alone, truly, was able to offer God.

A Glimmer at the Bottom of the Well?

THOMAS JOHNSON / 1986

THOMAS JOHNSON: *One gets the sense that you have been disappointed by the human race. When one watches your films, one is almost ashamed to be part of it. Is there still a glimmer at the bottom of the well?*

ANDREI TARKOVSKY: It's idiotic to talk about optimism or pessimism. These are senseless notions. People who cover themselves in optimism do it for political or ideological reasons. They don't want to reveal what they really think. Like the old Russian proverb says—a pessimist is a well-informed optimist. The position of the optimist is ideologically sly; it is theatrical and devoid of sincerity. By contrast, to hope is human. It's the state of being human. Humans are born with hope. One doesn't lose hope when faced with reality because hope is not rational. It is defended against all logic. Tertullian was right when he said, "I believe because it is absurd to believe." Hope has a tendency to grow in the face of the most sordid facts of real life. This is simply because horror, just like beauty, inspires a believer with hope.

TJ: *What are the dreams that have most marked you in life? Do you have visions?*

AT: I know a lot about my dreams. They are very important to me. But I don't like to reveal them. What I can tell you is that my dreams fall into two categories. There are prophetic dreams that come to me from

From *Nouvelles Clés*, October 21, 2003, from a previously unpublished interview conducted on April 28, 1986. Reprinted by permission of author. Translated from French by Deborah Theodore.

the transcendent world, from beyond. And there are random dreams that come from my contact with reality. Prophetic dreams come to me as I am falling asleep. When my soul separates from the plains of earth and rises to the summits of the mountain. Once man is away from the plains of the everyday he slowly begins to awaken. At the moment of awakening his soul is still pure and his dream images are full of meaning. It is these images brought back from on high that liberate us. But the problem is that these images very quickly become muddled with the images of the plains and become difficult to retrieve. What is certain is that up there time is reversible. Which proves to me that time and space only exist in the material incarnation. Time is not objective.

TJ: *Why do you dislike your film* Solaris? *Could it be that it is the only one of your films that is not sorrowful?*
AT: I think that the idea of consciousness is fairly well expressed in it. The problem is that there are too many pseudoscientific gadgets in the film. The orbiting space stations, the technology, all of that aggravates me enormously. Modern, technological contrivances are symbols to me of human error. Modern man is too preoccupied by his material development, by the pragmatic side of reality. He's like a predatory animal that doesn't know what to go after. Man's interest in a transcendent world has disappeared. Right now man is developing into a kind of earthworm: a tube that swallows up material and leaves little piles of waste behind him. Don't be surprised if one day the earth disappears because man has swallowed it all. What good is it to go out into space if it's only to distance ourselves from the fundamental problem of man: the harmonizing of the spiritual and the material world.

TJ: *Where do you stand on modernism?*
AT: Like a man with one foot on the bridge of one boat and one foot on the bridge of a second boat. One boat is going straight ahead and the other is turning right. Little by little I realize that I am falling into the water. Humanity is in this position right now. I see a very dim future if man does not realize that he's fooling himself. But I know that sooner or later he will realize. He can't just perish like a hemophiliac in his sleep, bleeding to death because he scratched himself before he

went to sleep. Art should be there to remind man that he is a spiritual being, that he is part of an infinitely larger spirit to which he will return in the end. If he's interested in these questions, if he simply asks himself these questions, he's already saved spiritually. It's not the answer that's important. I know that from the moment man begins asking the questions he will be unable to live as he has before.

TJ: *As strange as it seems, people who like your films also like Spielberg's science-fiction, and he's also fascinated by children. Have you seen his films, and what do you think of them?*

AT: By asking this question you demonstrate that you have no idea what you're talking about. Spielberg, Tarkovsky . . . it's all the same to you. Wrong! There are two kinds of filmmakers: those who see film as an art form and who ask themselves personal questions, who see the work as a kind of suffering, a gift, an obligation; and others who see it as a way to make money. That's commercial filmmaking. *E.T.*, for instance, is a story designed and created to please the greatest number of people. Spielberg accomplishes his goal with it, and so good for him. It's a goal that I have never looked to reach. For me all that is devoid of interest. Let's take an example—in Moscow there are ten million inhabitants, including tourists, and only three classical concert halls: the Tchaikovsky Hall and the grand and small halls of the Conservatory. Very little space and yet it satisfies everyone. Still no one says that music no longer plays a part in life in the USSR. In reality, the very presence of this great spiritual and divine art of music is enough. For me, populist art is absurd. Art is above all aristocratic. Musical art can only be aristocratic because at the moment of its creation it expresses the spiritual level of the masses, that to which they are unconsciously drawn. If everyone were capable of understanding it then masterpieces would be as common as the grass growing in the fields. There would not be this difference of potential that engenders the movement towards it.

TJ: *And yet in the USSR you are very popular. To see your films you have to fight for a ticket.*

AT: First of all, in the USSR I am considered a director who was forbidden, which excites the public. Secondly, I hope that the themes I am trying to express come from the depths of the soul, to the point that they become important to others as well as to me. Thirdly, my films are not a personal expression but a prayer. When I make a film, it's like a holy day. As if I were lighting a candle in front of an icon, or placing a bouquet of flowers before it. The spectator always ends up by understanding when you are sincere in what you are telling him. I don't invent any language to appear simpler, stupider, or smarter. A lack of honesty would destroy the dialogue. Time has worked for me. When people understood that I was speaking a natural language, that I wasn't pretending, that I didn't take them for imbeciles, that I only say what I think, then they became interested in what I was doing.

TJ: *Do you think like Solzenitsyn that the Western world is finished and that reality can only come from the East?*
AT: I am far from all these prophecies. Being Orthodox I consider Russia my spiritual home. I will never renounce it, even if I were never to see it again. Some say that the truth will come from the West, others say the East but, happily, history is full of surprises. In the USSR we are witnessing a spiritual and religious awakening. This can only be a good thing. But the third way is far from being found.

TJ: *What is on the other side of death? Do you have a feeling that you have traveled to this beyond? What have your visions been?*
AT: I believe in one thing: the human spirit is immortal and indestructible. In the beyond there could be anything, it is of no importance whatsoever. What we call death is not death. It's a rebirth. A caterpillar becomes a cocoon. I think there is life after death and it is that that is unnerving. It would be so much simpler to conceive of oneself as a telephone cord that is unplugged. Then you could live any way that you wanted. God would have no importance of any kind.

TJ: *When did you discover that you had a mission to accomplish and that it was your duty to humanity?*
AT: It is a duty to God. Humanity comes after. An artist collects and concentrates the ideas of the people. He is the people's voice. The rest is just work and service. My aesthetic and ethical position is defined by this duty.

TJ: *What is the last thing that you would like to say to mankind before leaving this earth?*

AT: The essence of what I have to say is in my films. It is impossible for me to get up on a rostrum that no one has built for me.

TJ: *In your book,* Sculpting In Time, *you say, "The West constantly cries out: Look! This is me! See how I suffer! How I love! Me! I! Mine! . . ." How have you resolved the problem of ego as a celebrated artist?*

AT: I still haven't solved this problem. But I have always had a feeling in myself of the influence and spell of Eastern culture. The Eastern man is called upon to offer himself as a gift to everything that exists. While in the West the important thing is to show yourself, validate yourself. This seems pathetic to me, naïve and animalistic, less spiritual and less human. In this sense I am becoming more and more Eastern.

TJ: *Why have you abandoned the filming of the life of Hoffman?*

AT: I haven't abandoned this film. I am postponing it until later. Making *The Sacrifice* was more important. The life of Hoffman was destined to be a romantic film. And romanticism is typically a Western phenomenon. It's a sickness. When a man gets older he sees his youth the way romantics look at life. The romantic era was spiritually rich but the romantics didn't know how to use their energy properly. Romantics embellish things, they do what I do when I don't feel as if I am enough for myself: I invent myself, I no longer create the world, I make it up.

TJ: *Why is it that in the beginning was the word, which happens to be the last sentence in* The Sacrifice?

AT: We misuse the word. It only has magical powers when it is the truth. Nowadays the word is used to conceal thoughts. In Africa there is a tribe that doesn't know what lying is. The white man tried to explain it but they didn't understand it. Try to understand the mystery of those souls and you will know why in the beginning was the word. The state of the word demonstrates the spiritual state of the world. Right now the gap between the word and what the word signifies is widening. It's very strange. It's an enigma!

TJ: *Are we living through the end of the world, or the end of a world?*

AT: Nuclear war? That wouldn't even be a victory for Satan. It would be like a child playing with matches and setting fire to the house. You can't even accuse it of pyromania. Spiritually man is not ready to survive his bombs. He's not mature enough. Mankind needs to study history. If there's one thing we've learned from history it's that it's never taught us anything. This is a very pessimistic conclusion. Mankind repeats its mistakes over and over again. It's horrible. Another enigma! I believe that we need to undertake some very important spiritual work in order for history to pass on to a more elevated level. . . . The most important thing is freedom of information; mankind should receive information without limits. It's the only positive tool. Unlimited truth is the beginning of freedom.

Faith Is the Only Thing That Can Save Man

CHARLES H. DE BRANTES/1986

AFTER HAVING TURNED DOWN numerous other solicita-
tions, as many from the French media as from the international
media, it's a very special gesture that the filmmaker wants to do for
France Catholique. His film *The Sacrifice* has just garnered four prizes
at the Cannes Film Festival: Grand Jury Prize, Prize for Best Artistic
Contribution, the International Critics Prize, and the Ecumenical
Jury Prize. A way for him to give thanks to all those who, throughout
this journal, have helped him to live in France with his family. The
announcement of his grave illness, against which he is nursing himself
at this moment, has caught the filmmaker off-guard, as much with
regard to the future plan of his life as in relation to new contracts he
was preparing to sign. Fatigue has prevented him from receiving everyone he would like to have seen.

The filmmaker is stretched out on his bed, wearing a house coat, in
front of a small fireplace which he was pleased to light. We're in the
seventeenth arrondissement of Paris, the evening falls, and we're going
to try to penetrate the Tarkovsky "mystery." We will find that it remains
intact. Happily perhaps.

Q: *Some folks have questioned the intertwining in your work, especially in*
The Sacrifice, *between Christian motifs, for example the recitation of the*
"Our Father," and ideas more archaic, more pagan, such as the character of

From *France Catholique*, no. 2060 (June 20, 1986). Reprinted by permission of author.
Translated from French by John Gianvito.

Maria, the "good witch." This leads to a certain confusion . . . Are you or are you not a Christian filmmaker?

T: I believe that it's truly not important to know if I subscribe to certain beliefs, whether pagan, Catholic, Orthodox, or simply Christian. The important thing is the work itself. It seems to me better to judge the work from a general perspective, and not to be searching for contradictions which some wish to see in my work. A work of art isn't always a mirror reflection of the inner world of the artist, particularly when it comes to the smallest of details. While it's true, there exists a certain logical connection . . . it's possible for there to be an opposition to the personal beliefs of the artist.

Also, when I directed this film, I was convinced it had to address itself to all types of audiences.

When I was very young I asked my father, "Does God exist—yes or no?" And he answered me brilliantly: "For the unbeliever, no, for the believer, yes!" This problem is very important.

I want to say in relation to this that it's possible to interpret the film in different ways. For instance, those who are interested in various supernatural phenomena will search for the meaning of the film in the relationship between the postman and the witch, for them these two characters will provide the principal action. Believers are going to respond most sensitively to Alexander's prayer to God, and for them the whole film will develop around this. And finally a third category of viewers who don't believe in anything will imagine that Alexander is a bit sick, that he's psychologically unbalanced as a result of war and fear. Consequently many kinds of viewers will perceive the film in their own way. My opinion is that its necessary to afford the spectator the freedom to interpret the film according to their own inner vision of the world, and not from the point of view that I would impose upon him. For my aim is to show life, to render an image, the tragic, dramatic image of the soul of modern man. In conclusion, can you imagine such a film being directed by a nonbeliever? I can't.

Q: *Some viewers also question the true faith of your characters. What is the essence of their beliefs? For instance, what was missing in Alexander's faith which would have helped him avoid insanity?*

T: Personally I don't consider Alexander to be insane. Undoubtedly there will be some spectators who believe he's gone mad. Quite simply I believe he is in a very difficult psychological state. He represents my idea of a certain type of individual. His inner world is that of a man who hasn't gone to church in a long time, who perhaps was educated by a Christian family, but who no longer believes in any traditional way, and perhaps no longer believes at all. I can envision him, for example, impassioned by Rudolf Steiner, with questions of anthroposophy . . . I can also imagine him as someone who is aware that the material world is not all there is, that there's a transcendent world waiting to be discovered . . . And when misfortune arrives, when the horror of a terrible catastrophe is imminent, he turns to God in a manner befitting his character, to the only hope which remains for him . . . It is a moment of despair.

Q: *Your characters always seem to remain on the threshold of a genuine spiritual life, in a sort of lasting innocence . . .*
T: Alexander, for me, despite the drama he is going through, is a happy man, because he has faith in the outcome of his circumstance. To me it seems a strange thing to say that he remains at the threshold of something given all he's lived through. . . . The most important and the most difficult religious problem is believing . . .

Q: *But this faith seems in a certain sense to border upon the absurd . . .*
T: That's only natural! For myself I think if someone is prepared to sacrifice himself, he can be called a believer. Of course, it's strange . . . Alexander sacrifices himself and at the same time demands that everyone else sacrifice themselves . . . it's a bit absurd. But what can one do? Without a doubt, in everyone's eyes he's lost; but that which is absolutely clear, is that he is saved.

Q: *In the opinion of some there is in* The Sacrifice *a certain Bergmanesque atmosphere. Do you acknowledge the Swedish director's influence or is it due to the spiritual atmosphere of the location where the film was shot?*
T: I don't agree at all. When Bergman speaks of God it's to say that he is silent, that he's not there. Hence, there can be no comparison with me. These are just superficial criticisms, saying this because the lead

actor also performs for Bergman, or because in my film there's a Swedish landscape, none of them having understood anything about Bergman. And they must not know what existentialism is, since Bergman is much closer to Kierkegaard than to the problem of religion.

Q: *Of all your films it seems that* The Sacrifice *is the most "theatrical." Could you imagine any of the scenes being staged for the theater?*
T: It's possible that it could be done, although I think it would be easier with *Solaris* or *Stalker*. But it's likely to be a poor spectacle, a bit pretentious. . . . Film interests me in that it pays no heed of the time or rhythm of the viewer, it has its very own. And if one was to transpose it to the stage, one eliminates this issue of the time I take in my film, which is something very important. Without it everything falls apart.

Q: *Your main actor, Erland Josephson, appears to be particularly concerned in his own personal life by the questions which excite you. Can you speak to us about your relationship?*
T: In fact the principal roles of the film were written especially for Erland Josephson and Allan Edwall. The rest came after.

Q: *How did you come to choose Valérie Mairesse?*
T: In the cinema, in general, we ruin actors. We use them, we humiliate them. I am very happy that Valérie Mairesse was able to play this little role. Professionals will see what lurks within her, what she's capable of doing. In practice, this was easy. Since France had contributed a significant sum of money to the production of the film, one of the clauses of the co-production was that it was necessary to hire a French actor, which is normal. I was offered about twenty actresses, and I chose Mairesse. She corresponded exactly to the character of Maillol that I'd been searching for, a countrywoman with a very solid disposition, very confident, and very pure. I am very grateful to her.

Q: *There is a tree which burns at the same time as the house at the end of* The Sacrifice. *Did that surprise you?*
T: There is never anything left to chance in my films. Why does the tree burn along with the house? If it had only been the house, it would have simply been another "film-fire," nothing real, nothing special . . .

Q: *It was a bit cruel . . .*

T: The tree was dead, it had been replanted, it was an element of the décor.

Q: *In* Nostalghia *you put into the mouth of the hero the words: "In our age, man should build pyramids." What type of pyramids did you have in mind?*

T: It's that man should aspire to spiritual greatness, he should leave behind him secrets that a million years from now others will need to decipher, not ruins which only bring to mind traces of catastrophe . . . I don't know . . . in any event not the nuclear plant at Chernobyl, just the opposite.

Q: *You said that you admired Robert Bresson. But isn't your cinema opposed to his? Bresson considerably pares down his images, and certain essential questions, he only sketches them, suggests them . . .*

T: In fact I consider Robert Bresson the best filmmaker in the world. I have only the greatest respect for him. Not counting that, I actually don't see many resemblances between us. He's able to cut down a shot in a way that I can't; it would be for me like killing a living being.

Q: *Someone just told me about a friend of theirs who was suicidal. He saw* The Sacrifice *and sat nearly two hours in rapt attention. He maintains that it revived his will to live.*

T: For me this is worth more than any opinion, any review. . . . The same thing happened to me after *Ivan's Childhood.* A criminal locked up in prison wrote me that he'd seen my film. He had experienced an inner transformation, he would no longer kill.

Q: *Why is it that so often in your films you have a scene of levitation, a body that rises in air?*

T: Quite simply because this is a scene with great potential. There are some things like this that are more cinematic, more photogenic. In the same way, water is very important to me. Water lives, it has a depth, it moves, it changes, it can be as reflective as mirror, one can drown within it, one can drink it, one can wash oneself with it, etc. Not to mention the fact that it's an indivisible molecule, that is, a monad.

Just as when I imagine someone who is able to fly, it pleases me . . . I find myself filled with emotion. If some fool asks me why in my last film people float up in the air, I'd tell him, "Because there's a witch." If someone with a more acute intelligence and poetic sensibility asks me, I would tell him that for these two characters, Alexander and Maria, love is not the same thing as it is for those who made *Betty Blue*.

Love is for me the supreme demonstration of mutual understanding, something that the representation of the sexual act can't express. In that case why not go film bulls atop cows out in the fields? Today everybody thinks it's censorship if one doesn't see "love" on screen. In reality this isn't love being shown but sex. The sexual act is for every one, for every couple, something unique. When it is put into films, it's the inverse.

Q: *Alexander's hesitation en route to Maria's house, which is a hesitation of his faith, and the one of Maria's in relation to her decision to sleep with Alexander, a hesitation of love—is it the same hesitation?*
T: The only way to show the sincerity of these two people was in find-ing a way to overcome the impossibility of there being any relationship between them. And in order to manage this, it was necessary that they be forced to surmount their differences . . .

Q: *How have you perceived your artistic evolution in making* The Sacrifice?
T: From the point of view of depth, of my penetrating into the world of modern man, I think I've succeeded better than in my previous films. But as far as the artistic, poetic value I consider *Nostlaghia* to be superior to *The Sacrifice*. Because *Nostalghia* is built on nothing, the film only exists insofar as the poetic image exists and that's all. Whereas *The Sacrifice* is based upon classical dramaturgy. For this reason I feel more attached to *Nostalghia*. I've always admired Bresson for his consistency, the coherent spirit that is carried throughout all his films. It's not an accident if the idea of consistency appeared in *The Sacrifice*, for instance, the glass of water poured every morning into the sink, the discussion of the system, etc. This is something very important for me. I hate leaving things to chance. Even the most poetic image, the most innocent, never happens by accident.

Q: *Stalker appears closest to* The Sacrifice . . .
T: In fact, *The Sacrifice* is the more consistent film for me. It's this need to be rational, to be consistent, that can drive man mad, and in this sense *The Sacrifice* is entirely incomparable to any of my other films.

Q: *Why have you chosen Saint Anthony as the subject of one of your next films?*
T: It's because it's important for me today to analyze a conflict which has always preoccupied man's spirit: what is holiness and what is sin? Is it such a good thing to be a saint? Because from an Orthodox view-point, communion is very important. For the Orthodox, the Church is the coming together of men united by the same beliefs, the same faith. But when the saint forsakes everything for the desert, why does he go? It's because he wants to save himself. But what's he to do about others? This question of the relationship between participation in life and per-sonal salvation preoccupies me a great deal.

Q: *But why the choice of Anthony?*
T: It could have been someone else. . . . The essential thing for me is the drama that man must pay for his attempts at balancing the spiritual life and the material life.

Q: *And why the Gospel According to Steiner as another future project?*
T: I never chose Steiner. Everyone asks me to make a film about him. To direct instead The Gospel According to Steiner is my way of reacting to these propositions. But I'm not convinced. That which interests me more are the people who wish for a solution, who are searching for an outlet. Those who proclaim to have found it . . . it seems to me that somewhere they're lying.

Q: *And why then a film about E. T. A. Hoffmann?*
T: Hoffmann, this is an old story. I had a great interest in him as a way of speaking about romanticism in general, and then to have done with him. If you recall the story of the life and death of Kleist and of his fiancé, then you'll know what I wanted to express. Romantics are people who have always tried to imagine life different than it was. The most terrible thing for them is routine, the daily habit, the relationship

to life as something fixed. Romantics are not fighters. When they perish, it's the result of chimeras they themselves created. For me romanticism as a way of looking at the world is very dangerous, where personal talent is regarded as something of capital importance. There are some more important things than that.

Q: *What are your precise relations with the Orthodox Church?*
T: Clearly, they are very difficult. I was formerly living in the USSR. I arrived in Italy, and now I live in France. Thus I unfortunately haven't had the opportunity to have a normal relationship with the Church. If I go to mass in Florence, the service is celebrated by a Greek, then by an Italian, but never by a Russian. It's the Orthodox Church, but Greek Orthodox or something. The only thing which has made a profound impression upon me recently was my meeting in London with Father Anthony Bloom. Some relationships with the Church demand a settled life, but I feel a little like someone underneath the debris after a bombardment . . . Hence it's pretty difficult for me to answer this.

Q: *It's said that the writer and Communist Party member Lounatcharski had wanted to emphasize in 1917 the religious character of the Revolution. What do you say about this?*
T: Where did he say that? What foolishness! Perhaps this was a way of justifying his admiration for the Revolution! I don't think that he said it, but when it was necessary to win popularity, people involved with NARKOM (The People's Committee for Education) would say and admit to anything!

Q: *You seem fascinated by the Apocalypse, as though you wanted to hasten its arrival . . .*
T: No. I'm quite simply looking at where we are . . . and since the Apocalypse is the Book about the End . . .

Q: *In his book,* The Visionaries, *Olivier Clément states that Nikolai Fyodorov felt that traditional individual asceticism could be made collective and transform the cultural landscape completely. What do you think about that?*
T: If the world was capable of being turned around by asceticism, by inner effort, than why has four thousand years of civilization come

186 ANDREI TARKOVSKY: INTERVIEWS

to such a catastrophic result? For two thousand years it was necessary
to have Golgotha to set humanity in the right direction. But men
haven't heeded this. I realize it's harmful to think that this served no
purpose . . . although, in a certain sense, it helped . . . man aspired to
heights. If there hadn't been that, truly there wouldn't have been
anything.

Q: *I noticed several times that you were reading Berdyaev. Do you consider
yourself a disciple of his?*
T: No, not at all. I don't agree with all his opinions. He approaches
problems as if he's above them, as if he's resolved them. I don't believe
people like that, like Steiner, or Berdyaev. Otherwise I'd have to believe
that there existed men who possessed innate knowledge. This isn't
possible.

Q: *Yet Christians sometimes express themselves by saying that Christ is the
only solution . . .*
T: Faith is all that man truly possesses. When Voltaire said "If God
didn't exist, it would be necessary to invent him," he didn't say this
because he didn't believe, he had a strong faith, that's not the reason.
Materialists and Positivists took Voltaire's words and gave it a bad con-
notation. Faith is the only thing that can save man, that's my deepest
conviction. Otherwise what can one do? It's the only thing that inar-
guably belongs to one. Everything else has no reality.

Q: *What's your interpretation of Dostoevsky's phrase, "Beauty will save the
world"?*
T: There have been a lot of speculations, oftentimes vulgar, attributed
to this expression. Certainly when Dostoevsky spoke of beauty, he was
referring to spiritual purity. This is the case with Prince Myshkin and
Rogozhin, but not with the physical beauty of Nastasia Filipovna,
which was, in fact, cheap, unkempt . . .

Q: *You've said that man should create in the image and likeness of the
Creator . . .*
T: It's all together important and not important. For me, it's like
breathing in air . . .

Q: *But how do you distinguish the artist from the monk and from the saint?*
T: These are truly different paths. The saint, the monk, refuses to create because he's not participating in life. The banner of the saint or the monk is non-participation. This has a lot in common with Buddhist and Oriental philosophy. . . . But the artist, the poor artist . . . he finds himself again in the mud amidst everything that happens. But we also know about the example of the French poet who rejected being a poet, Rimbaud. There are a lot of people like that.

For the monk, I feel a sort of compassion, because he lives with only part of himself. As for the artist, he has a tendency to scatter himself, to make mistakes, to sully himself, jeopardizing his soul. But this isn't to characterize the saint and the poet as angel and devil. It's quite simply people who find themselves in some very dissimilar situations. The saint will have salvation. The artist perhaps not. In this sense I believe in the grace which descends upon you from above, just like that . . . Herman Hesse had this thought: "All my life I aspired to be a saint, but I am a sinner. I can only count on inspiration from on high." What he's saying is that he's unable to be consistent.

There's a parallel between the saint and artist, but there are some different problems. . . . The essential thing is that one live in a just and proper way. Seeking to imitate the Creator, or seeking his salvation. Saving oneself, or searching to create a far richer spiritual climate for the entire world.

Who knows how much time remains for any of us? One must live thinking that tomorrow we may have to deliver our soul up to God. You ask me a question to which some geniuses have dedicated their whole life. That's what it is to make a film. I want to speak to this in my film about Saint Anthony, in order to understand and explain this unbearable problem for man. In the end to die or not to die isn't a problem, we all will die, either together or one after the other . . .

INDEX

CONVERSATIONS WITH FILMMAKERS SERIES
PETER BRUNETTE, GENERAL EDITOR

The collected interviews with notable modern directors, including

Robert Aldrich • Woody Allen • Pedro Almodóvar • Robert Altman •
Theo Angelopolous • Bernardo Bertolucci • Tim Burton • Jane Campion •
Frank Capra • Charlie Chaplin • The Coen Brothers • Francis Ford Coppola •
George Cukor • Brian De Palma • Clint Eastwood • Federico Fellini •
John Ford • Terry Gilliam • Jean-Luc Godard • Peter Greenaway • Howard
Hawks • Alfred Hitchcock • John Huston • Jim Jarmusch • Elia Kazan •
Stanley Kubrick • Fritz Lang • Spike Lee • Mike Leigh • George Lucas •
Sidney Lumet • Roman Polanski • Michael Powell • Jean Renoir • Martin
Ritt • Carlos Saura • John Sayles • Martin Scorsese • Ridley Scott • Steven
Soderbergh • Steven Spielberg • George Stevens • Oliver Stone • Quentin
Tarantino • Lars von Trier • Liv Ullmann • Orson Welles • Billy Wilder •
John Woo • Zhang Yimou • Fred Zinnemann

CPSIA information can be obtained
at www.ICGtesting.com
Printed in the USA
BVHW072125100922
646366BV00001B/33

9 781578 062201